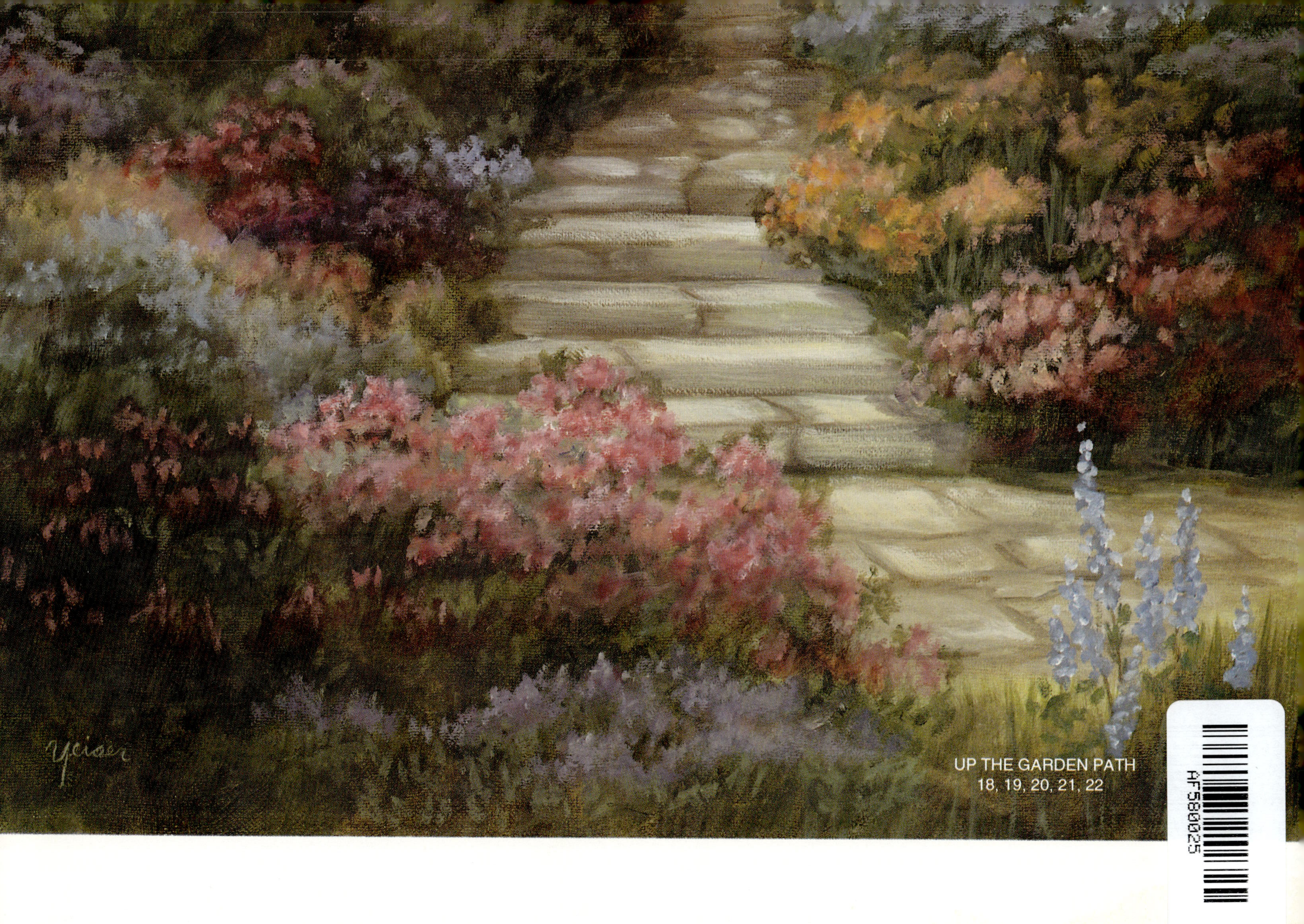

UP THE GARDEN PATH
18, 19, 20, 21, 22

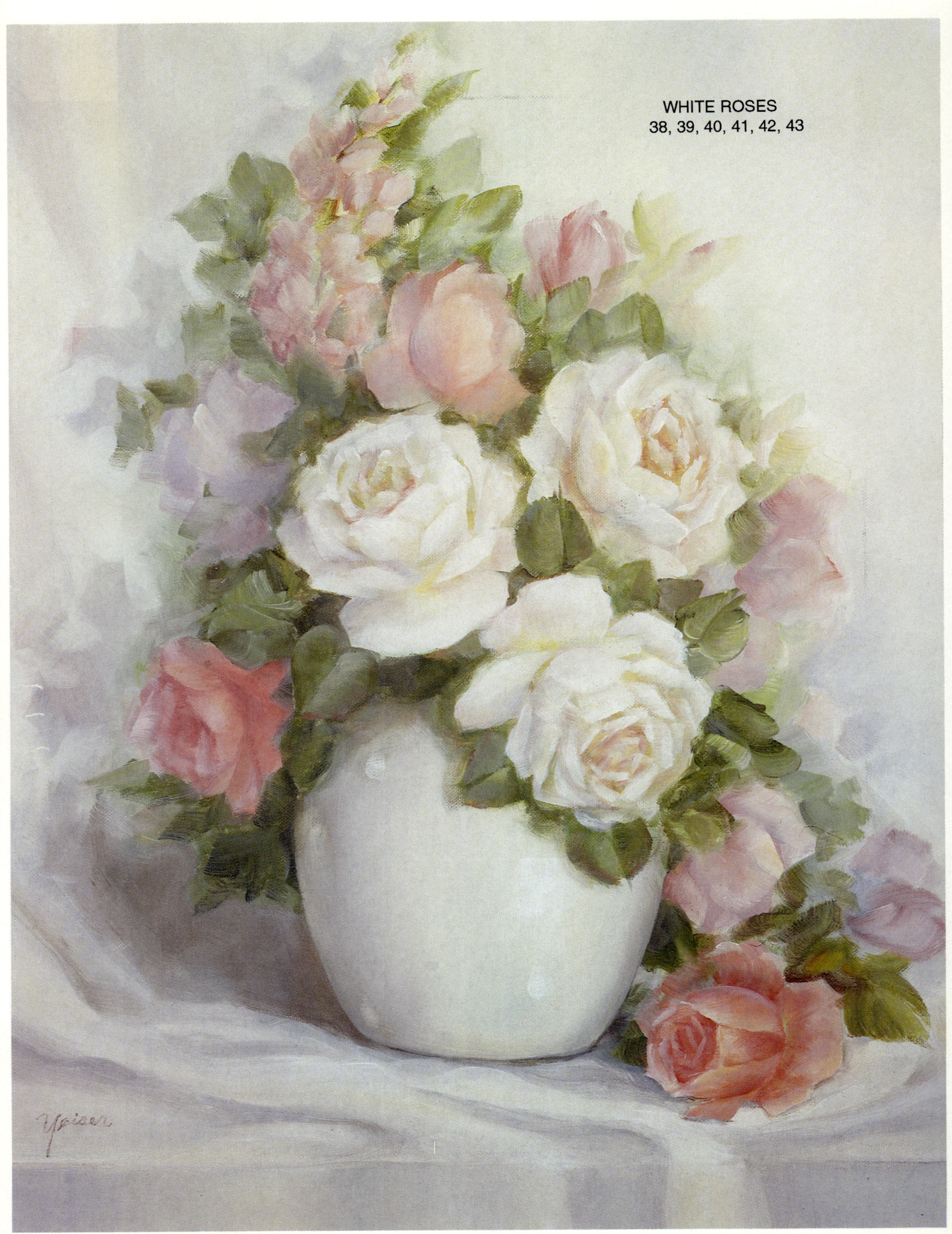

WHITE ROSES
38, 39, 40, 41, 42, 43

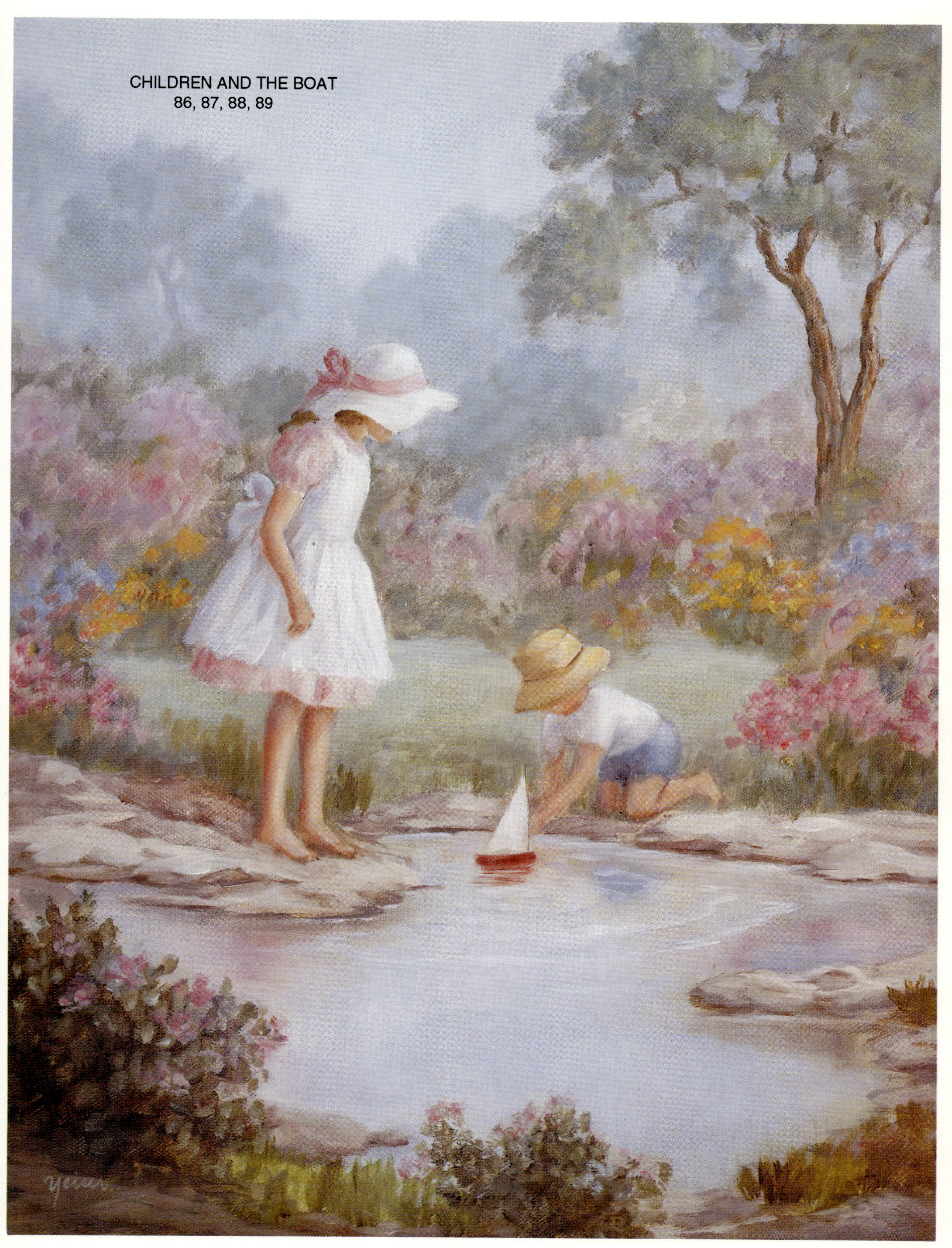

CHILDREN AND THE BOAT
86, 87, 88, 89

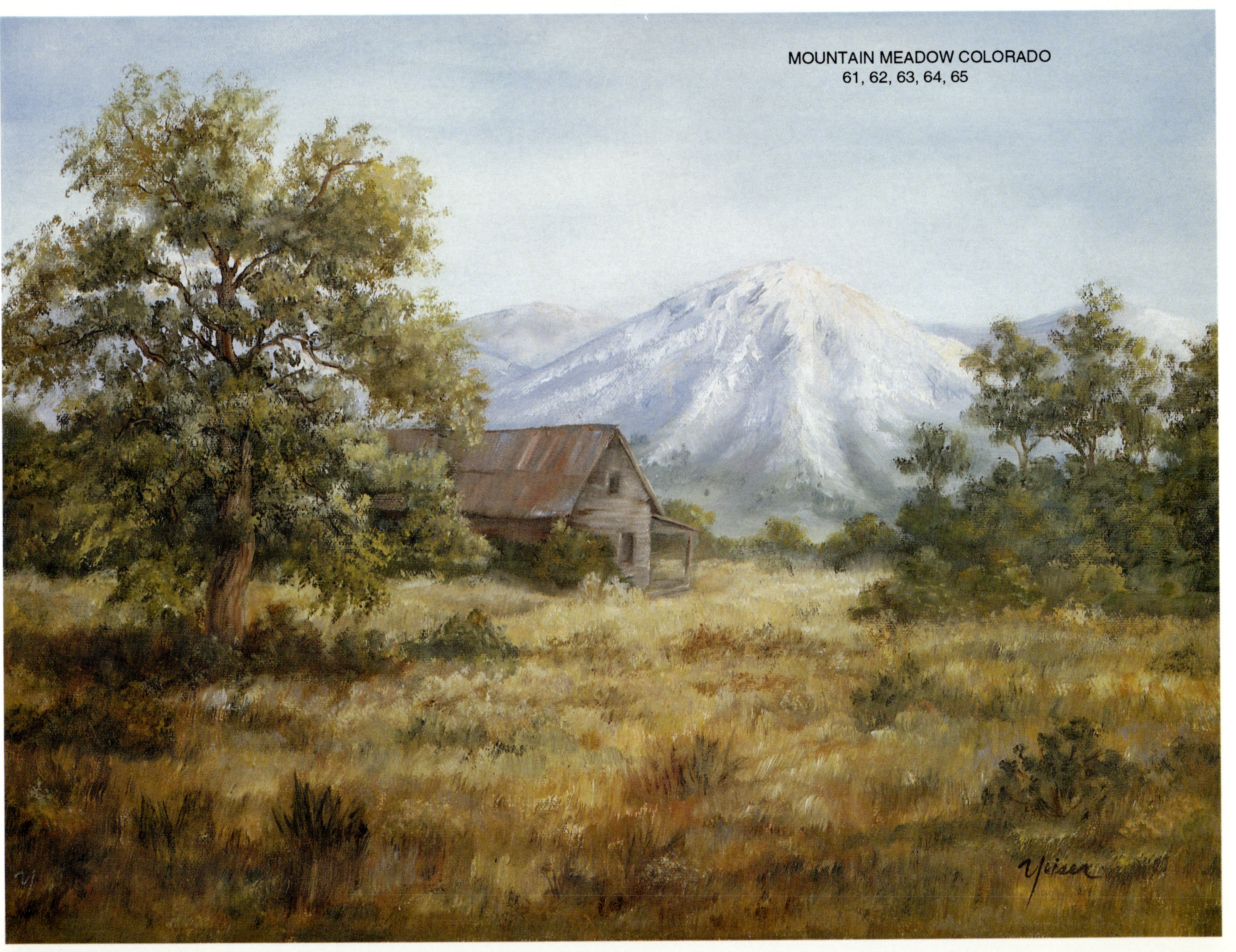

MOUNTAIN MEADOW COLORADO
61, 62, 63, 64, 65

ABOUT THE AUTHOR

Mildred Yeiser was born in Kentucky, but moved to Houston, Texas in 1958 with her family. She enjoys traveling, photography and collects porcelain birds.

She became interested in art while in college and later went on to study with a number of teachers. She was privileged to attend art seminars and lectures at the Victoria and Albert Museum and the National Gallery in London, England.

Her work has been shown in a number of galleries in the United States and private collections in Europe.

She has taught classes and workshops for the past fifteen years.

DEDICATION

My Thanks to my family for their patience and support, to Susan Scheewe for her confidence and to my daughter Nancy for typing Thanks especially to my husband and son, Norman and Joseph Daniel Yeiser for their contribution of landscape photography.

NOTES

Read all directions before you start a picture.

MEDIUM

Avoid using too much medium. This is a common problem. When the word medium is used it means, Stand Oil Light or Linseed Oil Light plus a small amount of turpentine. (L.O.T.) Add 1 tablespoon of turpentine to 4 oz. of linseed. Shake well.

PRIME

There are many ways to prepare canvas for painting. Wiping a canvas with turpentine tinted with a small amount of pigment is an easy way. You see color more easily on colored canvas. Also, pinholes in the surface are filled. Turpentine evaporated rapidly so you won't have to wait long before you can paint.

BRUSHES

I use both red and Royal Sable flats. I like Royals because they have the right amount of body for my purposes. Each artist will develop their own preference.

When painting roses your brush must be in good condition for best results. That is it must paint to a knife edge and be soft.

Fan brushes referred to in this book are bristle brushes. Softer fan brushes are good for blending but not for painting.

RULER

It is easier to work with a clear plastic ruler since you can see through it. This helps you to relate to the lines covered by the ruler. Long rulers are better for long lines.

PALETTE

It helps to arrange your palette in the same order each time you paint. Put the white, yellows, reds, blues in the same places. Work out a system that is handy for you.

Permalba Brilliant Yellow Light - This is a warm white. Other brands of this color are very nice for other things but I used this brand for its warmth.

Winsor Newton Sap Green - This is my favorite Sap Green. It covers better and works well for me.

SUPPLIES

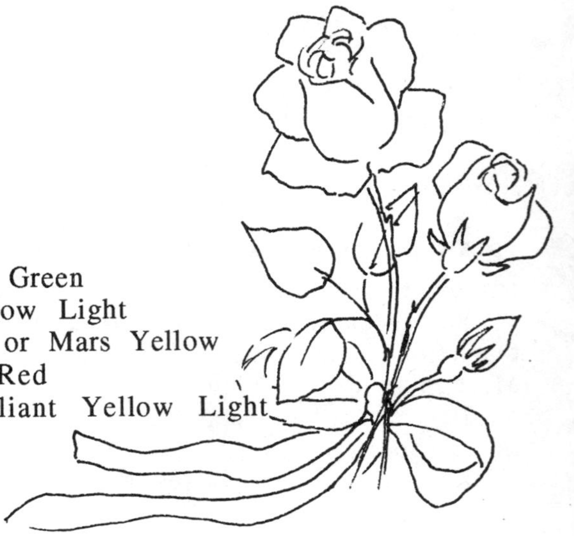

OIL PAINT

Titanium White
Cobalt Blue
Ultramarine Blue
Cerulean Blue
Indigo
Paynes Gray
Cadmium Red Light
Alizarine Crimson
Sap Green
Viridian Green
Unbleached Titanium

Raw Umber
Burnt Umber
Raw Sienna
Burnt Sienna
Thalo Yellow Green
Cadmium Yellow Light
Yellow Ochre or Mars Yellow
Grumbacher Red
Permalba Brilliant Yellow Light
Parchment

BRUSHES

Flat Sables 1 inch or #44, 32, 28, 22, 20, 18, 16, 12, 10, 6, 4, 2
Bristle Fan Brush 1, 2, and 5
Spotter 1
Stippler 1/4 and i/2 Inch
Liner 1, 2

MEDIUM

Stand Oil Light or Linseed Oil and Turpentine mixed L.O.T.

OTHER SUPPLIES

18 inch clear plastic ruler
Palette Knife with small rounded end

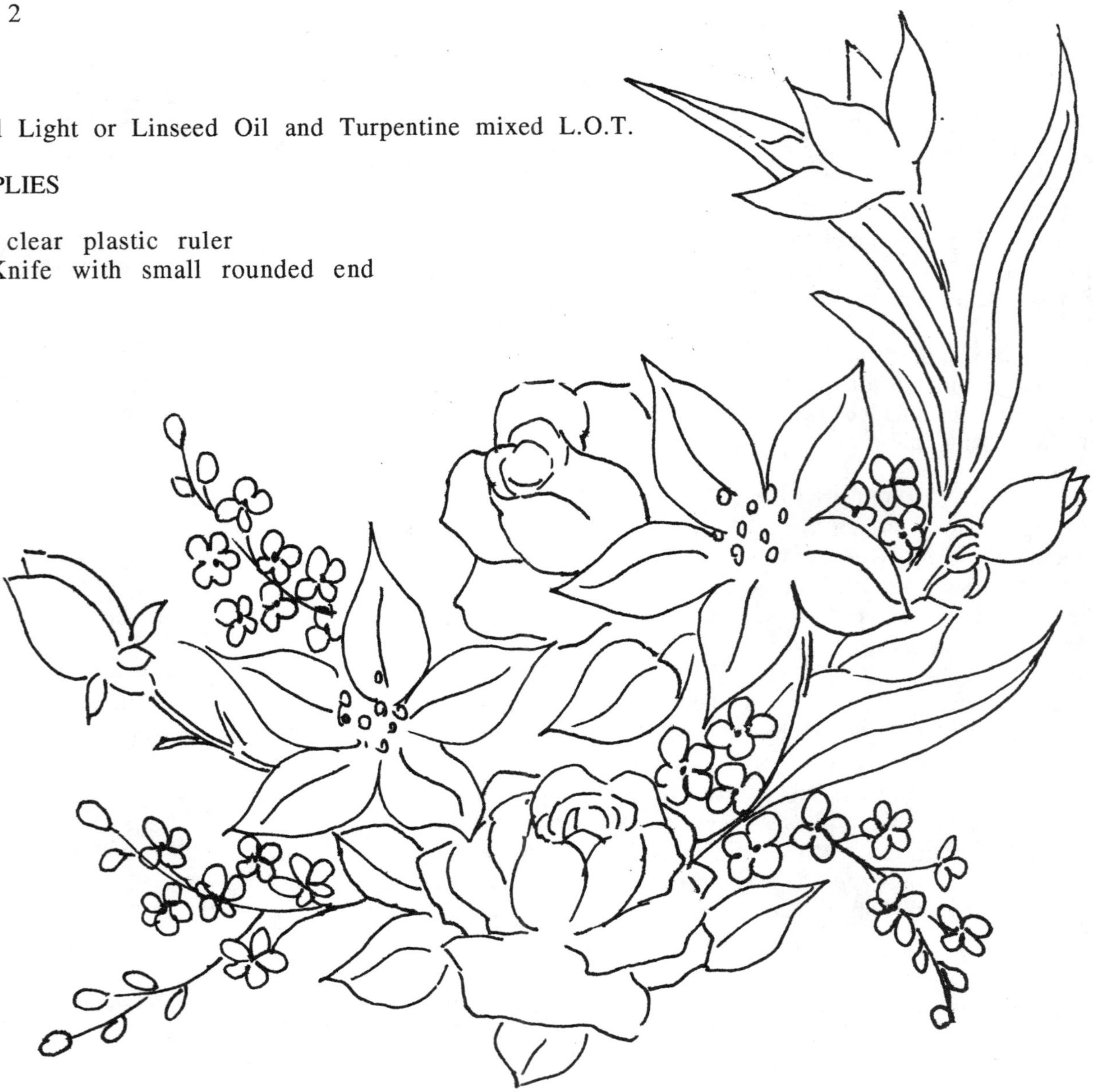

MIXED FLOWERS

LEAVES

Mix the following colors:
Deep Green: Sap Green and Cobalt Blue
Medium Green: Sap Green and Cadmium Yellow Light
Light Cool Green: Sap Green, Cobalt Blue and White
Light Yellow Green: Sap Green, Cadmium Yellow Light and White

Use a #32 flat brush brush. These leaves are very casual and unformed. Most are simply a flat stroke drawn at an angle. Some are dabs or smudges. See the color illustration for placement.

FLOWERS

PINK LILIES- Mix the following:
Light Pink: Grumbacher Red and White
Rose: Alizarin Crimson and White

Cover the petals with light pink allowing some of the green prime to show in the center. Use a #18 flat brush .

Brush out from the center with some of the rose color.

Mix some Alizarine Crimson and turpentine to make a thin liquid paint. Splatter the spots with a stiff brush. This brush can be a bristle fan brush or even an old tooth brush.

Use a #2 flat to draw in the center lines on each petal.

Add ruffles on the edges with Brilliant Yellow Light using a #4 flat brush. Use a #2 liner to put in the small green lines in the center. A dab of Burnt Sienna and Cool Red Light will do for the brown dots. Use the liner for this. Not know the scientific names for flower parts they will just have to be green lines and brown dots.

The same pinks are used for the other pink flowers.

PEACH ROSES- Mix the following:
Dark Peach: Grumbacher Red, Cadmium Red Light and White
Light Peach: Add more White to the above.

Use a #32 flat brush and broad strokes for the rose petals. Use the dark peach for underpainting.

Some medium will be necessary for the lighter top petals.

Apply over the wet underpainting. Don't use up all the dark color. Losing your darks is a real problem in flower painting.

All strokes should move toward the stem. Highlight while wet with Brilliant Yellow Light tinted with peach.

For variations on the peach colors add more yellows or white.

Some flowers are just bright blobs. When painting mixed bouquets like this one every thing doesn't have to be a specific kind of flower.

WHITE SNAPDRAGONS

Put darker background colors in the area of the blossoms. This dark should be dark enough to frame out the Brilliant Yellow Light.

Add the stems using shades of green. A #4 flat brush is good for this. The top most snapdragon has some of the Thalo Yellow Green showing and some lavender tones on the left side. The one on the table is also shadowed. Use a #18 flat brush to add Brilliant Yellow Light for highlights.

VASE

Paint everything inside the glass first. Put in smudges of green leaves, reflected pinks and peach and some lavender from the shadows. Use a #28 flat brush for this.

Put in the stems with a #16 flat. Zigzag across them to distort.

Draw a dark lavender line under the vase. Use light yellow to draw in the sides and bottom line. The left side line is broken.

The reflected light on the bottom is brighter on the left.

Add highlights with White a #18 flat brush. Add a second highlight on top of the first for sparkle

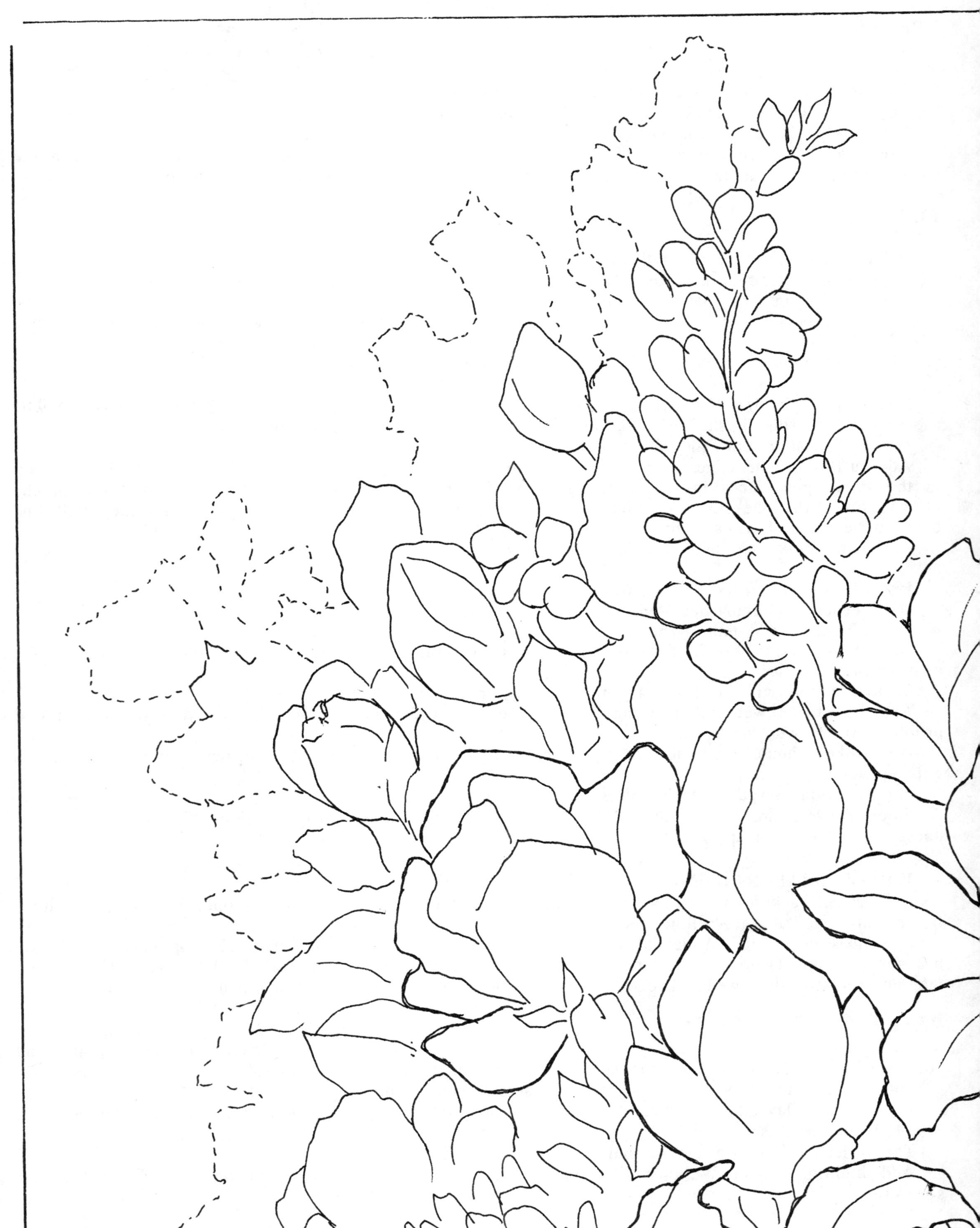

MIXED FLOWERS

PALETTE
White
Cadmium Yellow Light
Brilliant Yellow Light
Mars Yellow
Cadmium Red Light
Grumbacher Red
Alizarin Crimson
Thalo Yellow Green
Sap Green
Cobalt Blue
Raw Umber
Burnt Sienna

BRUSHES
Flat Sables #44, 32, 22, 18, 16, 42
Liner #2
Bristle Fan Brush

MEDIUM Stand Oil or L.O.T.
Turpentine

CANVAS: 16 x 20

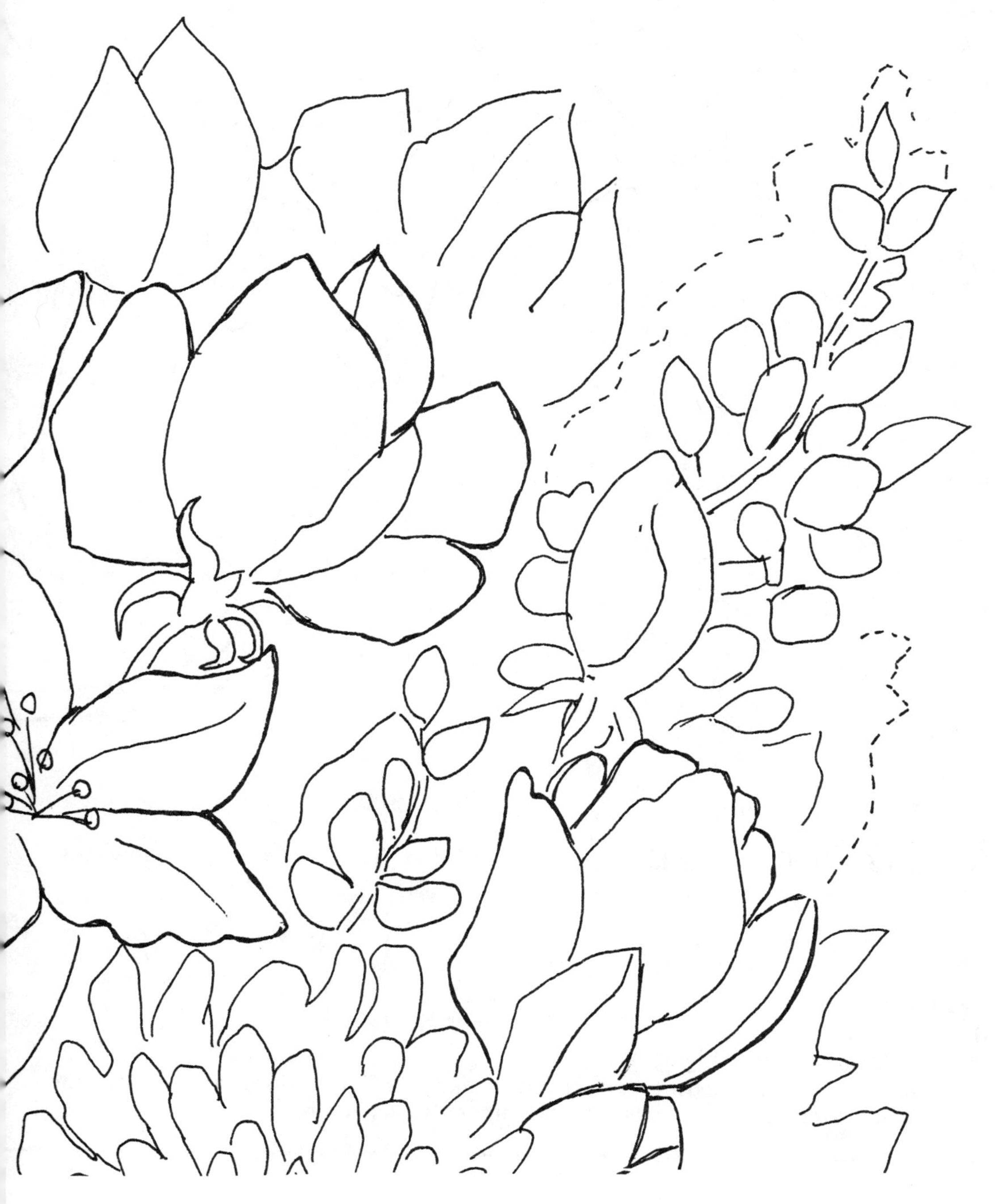

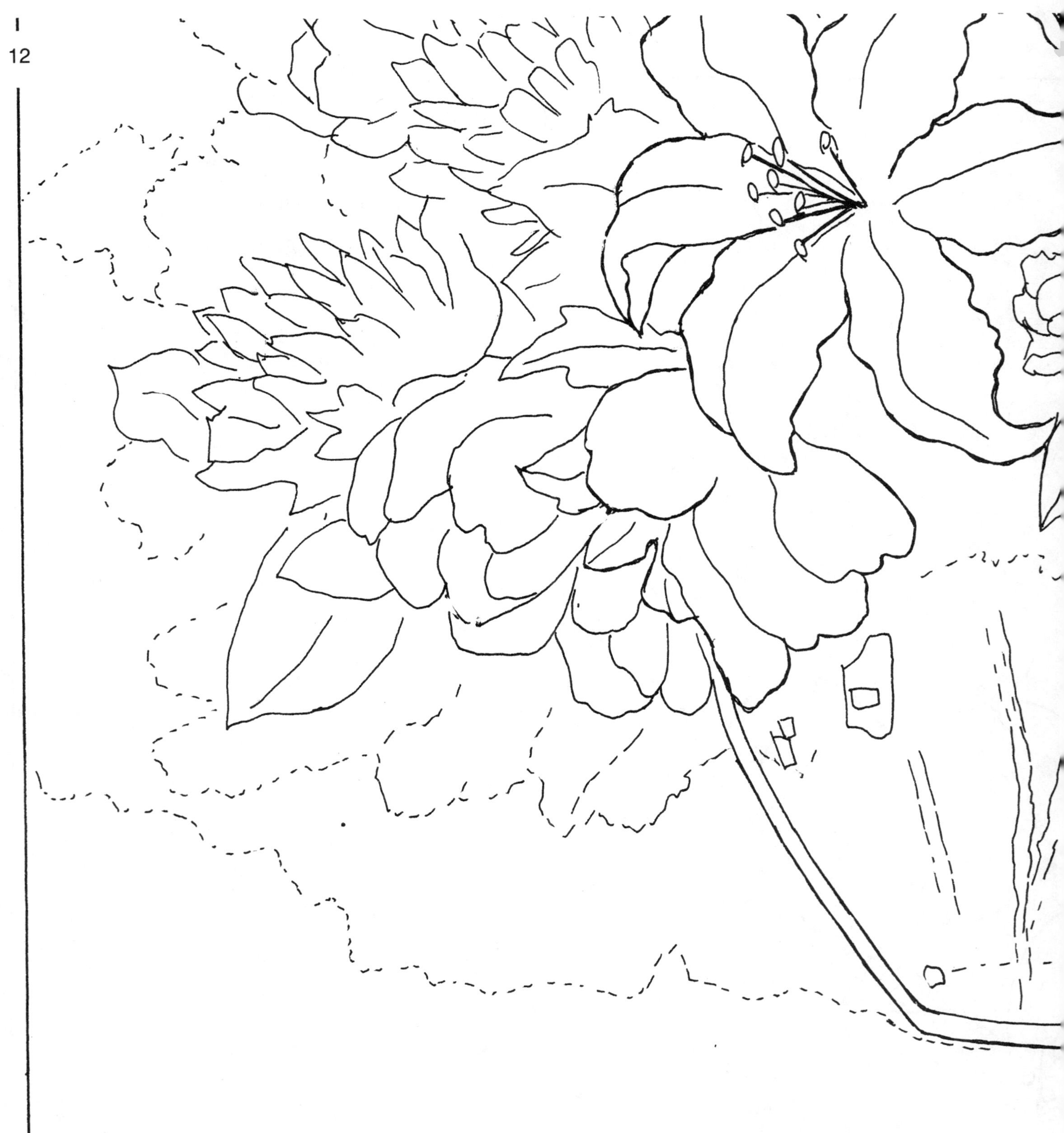

Prime the canvas with turpentine tinted to a light green using Thalo Yellow Green. Allow this to dry.

BACKGROUND

Mix the following:
Off White: Raw Umber and White
Light Yellow: White, Mars Yellow
Deep Lavender: Cobalt Blue, Cadmium Red Light, White

With a #44 brush put in the background using crisscross strokes. The colors above are the basic background colors but as you paint, work in bits of the other flower colors.

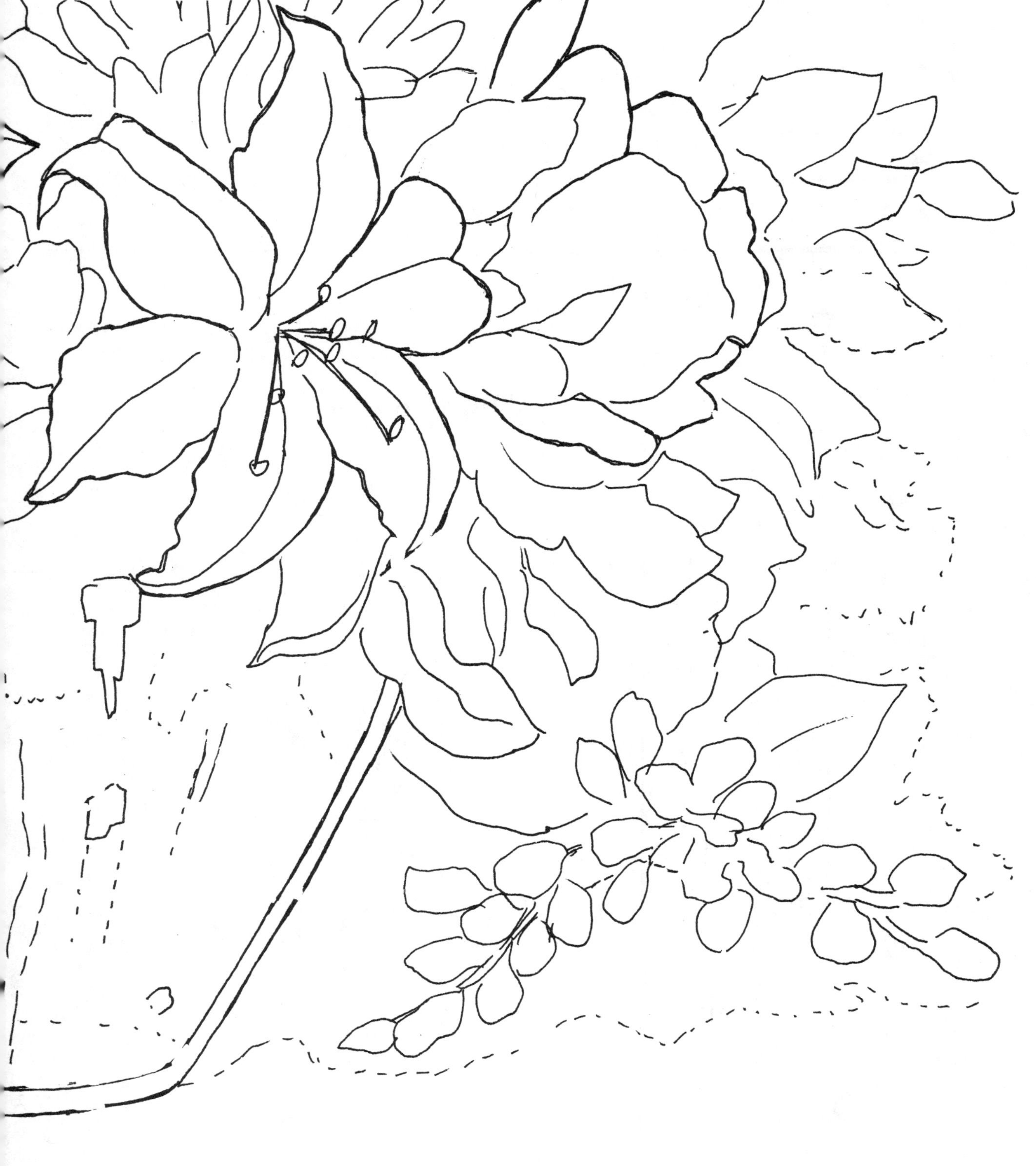

The deep lavender is in back of the vase and worked into the left side. It will be lighter toward the top left side. Use the same colors in front of the vase on the folds of the table cloth. Some medium will be necessary.

For the shadow leaves use the lighter lavender areas on the left. Draw around leaf shapes using the flat of the brush and one of the lighter background colors.

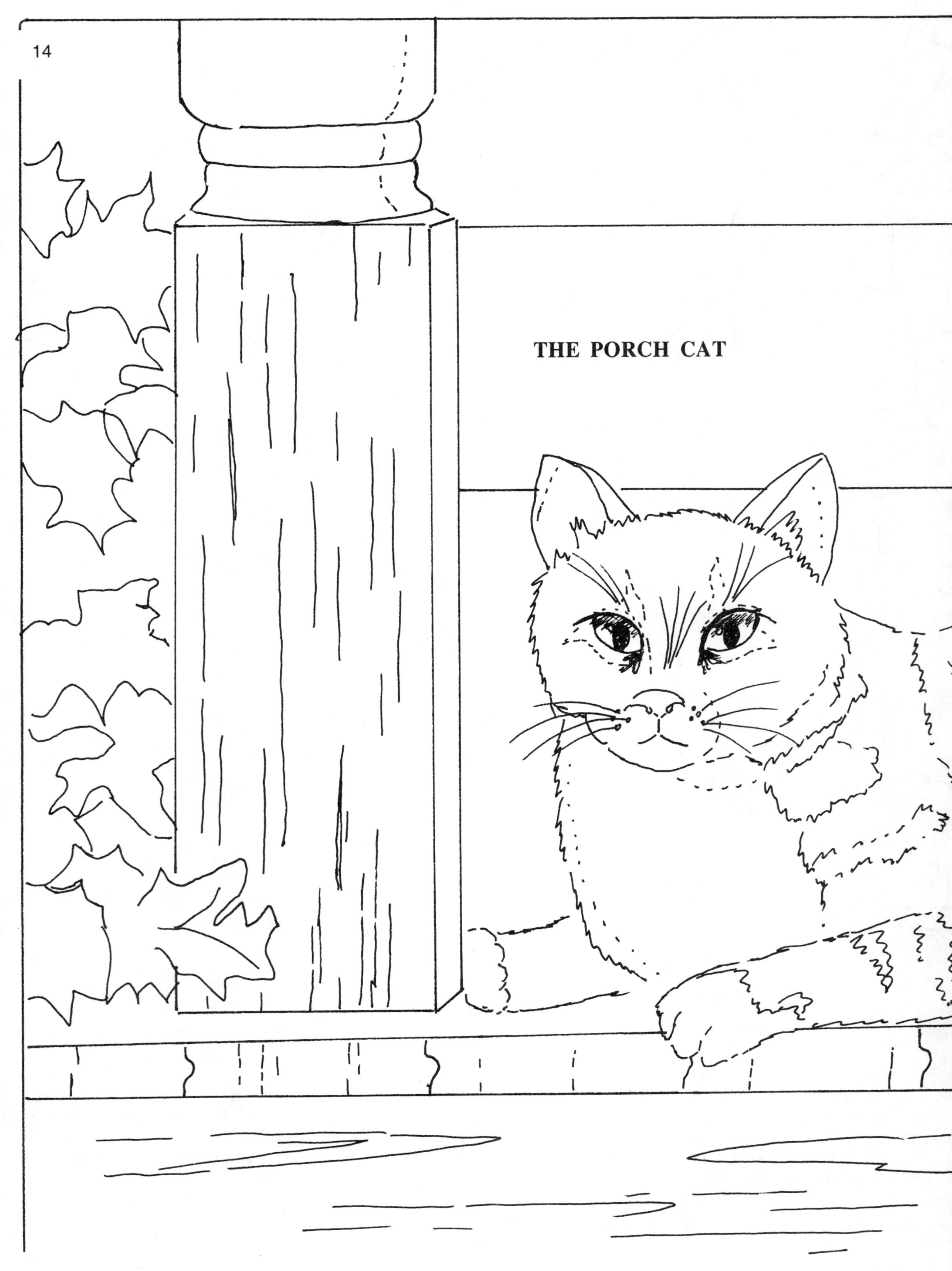
THE PORCH CAT

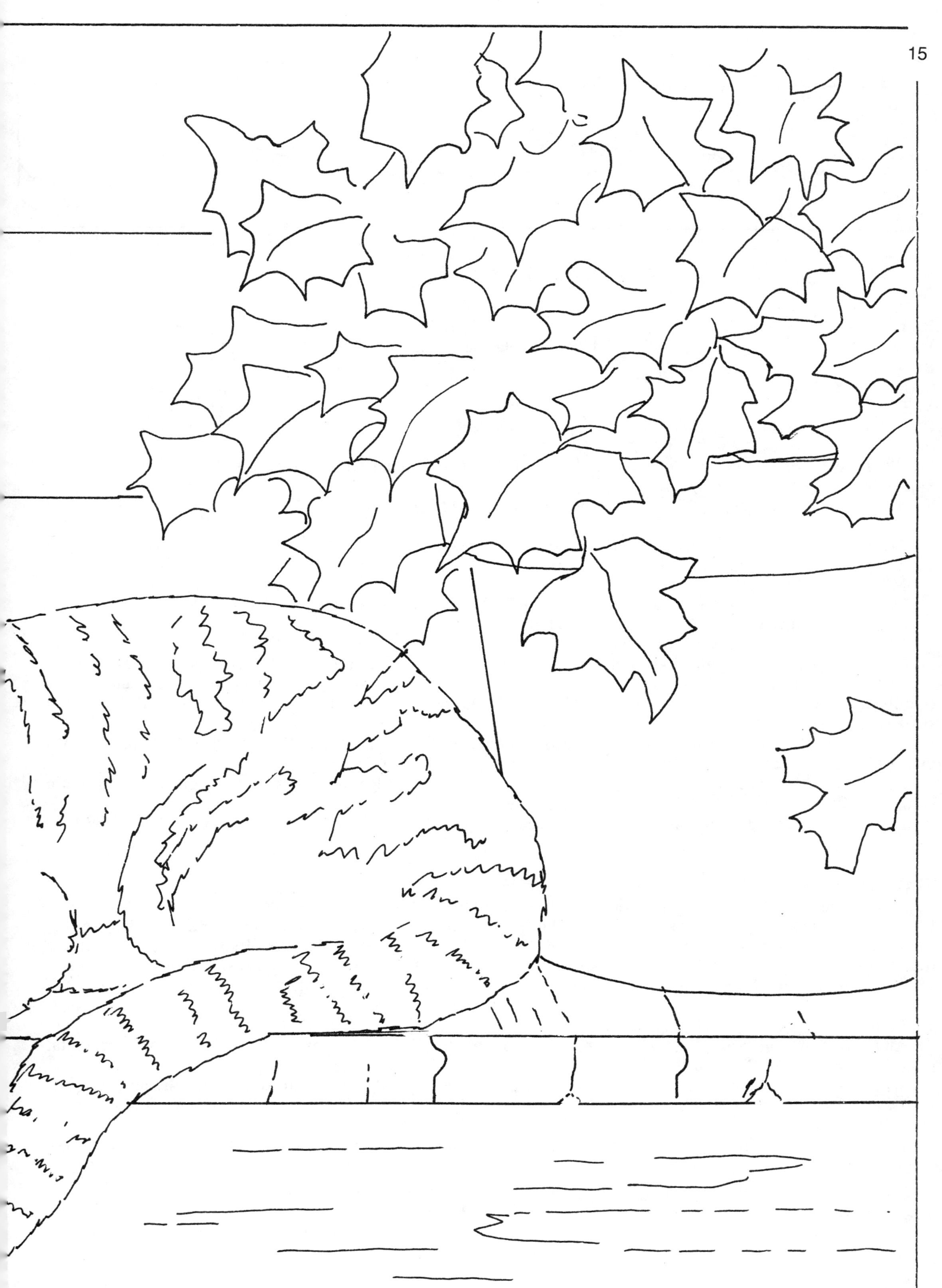

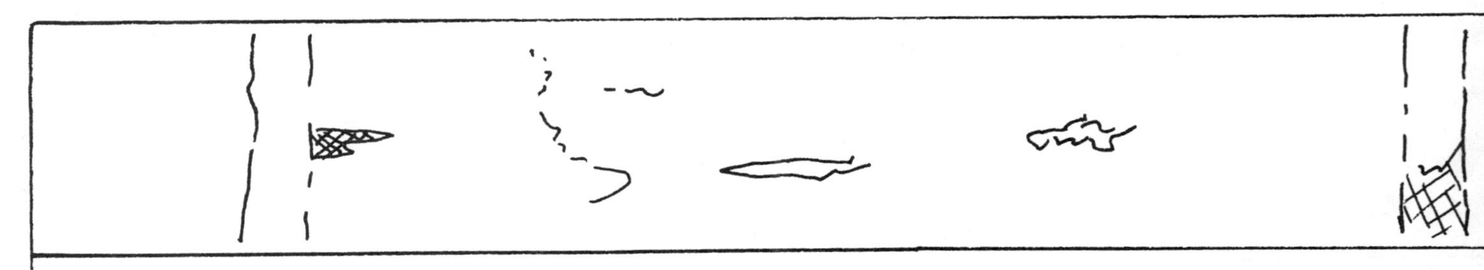

THE PORCH CAT

PALETTE
White
Brilliant Yellow Light
Cadmium Yellow Light
Yellow Ochre
Cadmium Red Light
Paynes Gray
Cobalt Blue
Sap Green
Raw Umber

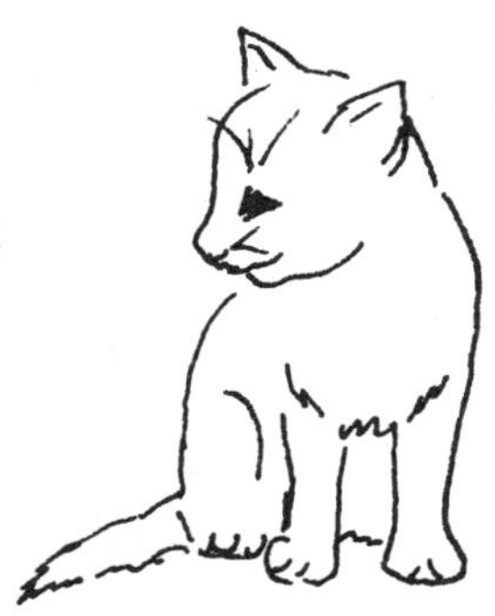

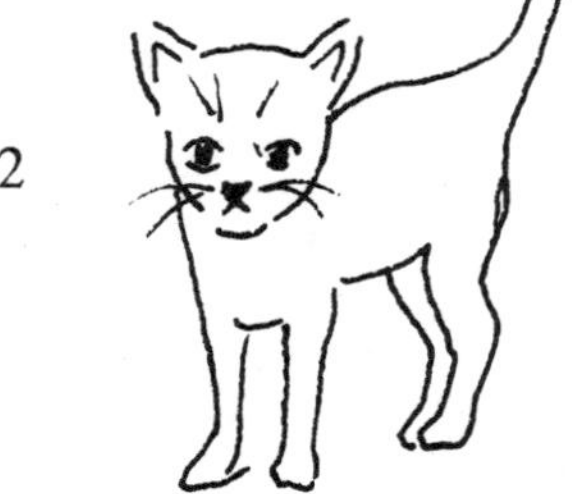

BRUSHES
Flat Sable 32, 28, 16, 12, 4, 2
Bristle Fan Brush #1
Blender, small or medium
Liner # 2
Spotter #1

MEDIUM: Stand Oil Light or L.O.T.

CANVAS: 12 x 16

Trace pattern on the canvas. Prime the dark areas of the cat with turpentine tinted with Raw Umber.

Mix the following:

Dark Neutral Gray: Cobalt Blue, Cadmium Red Light, Yellow Ochre

Medium Neutral Gray: Add White to the dark gray

Dark Brown: Raw Umber with a bit of White

Paint the area behind the cat with medium gray. Use a #32 brush and crisscross strokes.

Add White to the medium gray to make a lighter gray to cover the past, porch edge and facing (the board above the bricks). Use vertical strokes with a #28 flat brush for the post and horizontal strokes on the facing.

Put in the shadows on the side of the post and under the edge of the floor with a @18 brush. Do this while the base paint is still wet.

Add streaks of dark brown for the wood grain using the edge of the #18 flat brush. Wood grain is made with a light stroke. Don't get too detailed.

Use dark gray and dark brown for the cracks, rings, shadows and distress marks. The #2 and #4 flat brushes are good for the details.

FLOWER POT

Mix a basic rust color using Raw Umber, Cadmium Red Light and White. Cover the flower pot. Use a #28 brush and crisscross strokes. While the paint is wet work in some Raw Umber in the shadows and under the rim. Add some Cadmium Yellow Light to the lightest area to create roundness. Add White in vertical stripe and work it in with crisscross strokes. This should be a very soft highlight. These pots do not have a hard highlight. Use a little medium as necessary.

BRICKS

Add Whit to the rust to make a rosey color or the bricks. Cover the brick using horizontal strokes with a #28 flat brush.

While the rose color is wet work in some Raw Umber for shadows and some Sap Green for moss. Use crisscross strokes for this. With the #2 and #4 brushes add cracks , holes and flaws with a little Raw Umber. A few dabs of medium gray adds interest.

Use medium gray for the mortar. Use a #4 flat brush. Blend the edges a bit so they won't be too sharp.

This type of still life is sometimes improved by working it more than once. Study a piece of weathered wood and some old bricks and enjoy the details.

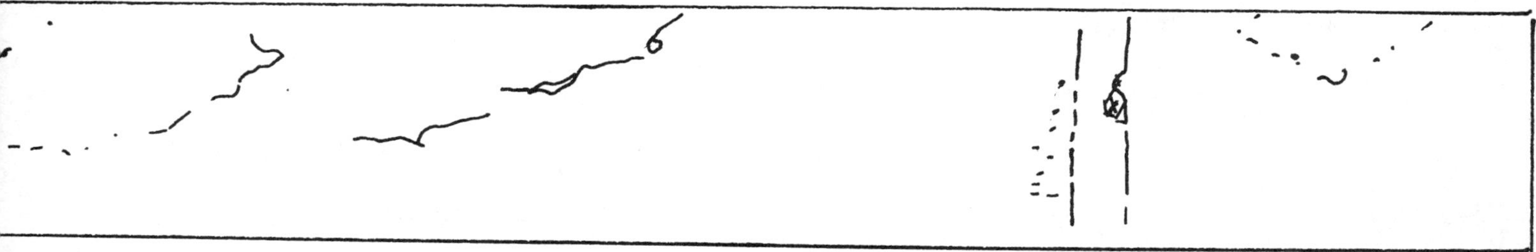

CAT

Mix a warm black using Paynes Gray and Raw Umber (not a true black but it matched the Cat). Add some White to make a medium gray. On some of the stripes I added some Yellow Ochre to the medium gray. This cat may have had a calico ancestor. He looks slightly stupefied due to a whole can of tuna.

Use the #2 fan brush to apply the hair. If you cut off the corners of the brush it will be easier to use.

Put in alternate stripes using the black and gray. Pull the strokes in the direction the hair grows. Add the dark areas of the face with a #12 flat brush.

Cover the white areas and shade them with some of the medium gray using a #16 flat brush. Highlight the white areas with Brilliant Yellow Light. When the whole cat is covered blend while it is still wet. Use a small to medium blender. The strokes should follow the natural direction of the hair. Allow the cat to dry before doing the details.

EYES

Mix some White with Yellow Ochre to make a light yellow for the iris. Add a dab of Cadmium Yellow Light to add sparkle. Use a #2 flat brush. Put in the black pupils and a dot for the highlight. Give him some black eyeliner.

NOSE

Mix White and rust to make a dark pink for the nose. Use the #2 flat brush for the details. Brush a little of the pink on the inside ears/ Put in dots of Raw Umber on each side of his nose for bases of the whiskers.

Add the whiskers with turpentine to a liquid consistency so that the liner will carry it. Practice a few stroke before you do the cat.

IVY

Cover the leaves with Sap Green. You may add a bit of Cobalt Blue in the cool shadow areas.

Mix Sap Green, Cadmium Yellow Light and White to highlight a few leaves on the front, light side. A bit of rust color can be added to relieve the greenness. See the color illustration.

Now you are finished, I hope you enjoy this as much as I did.

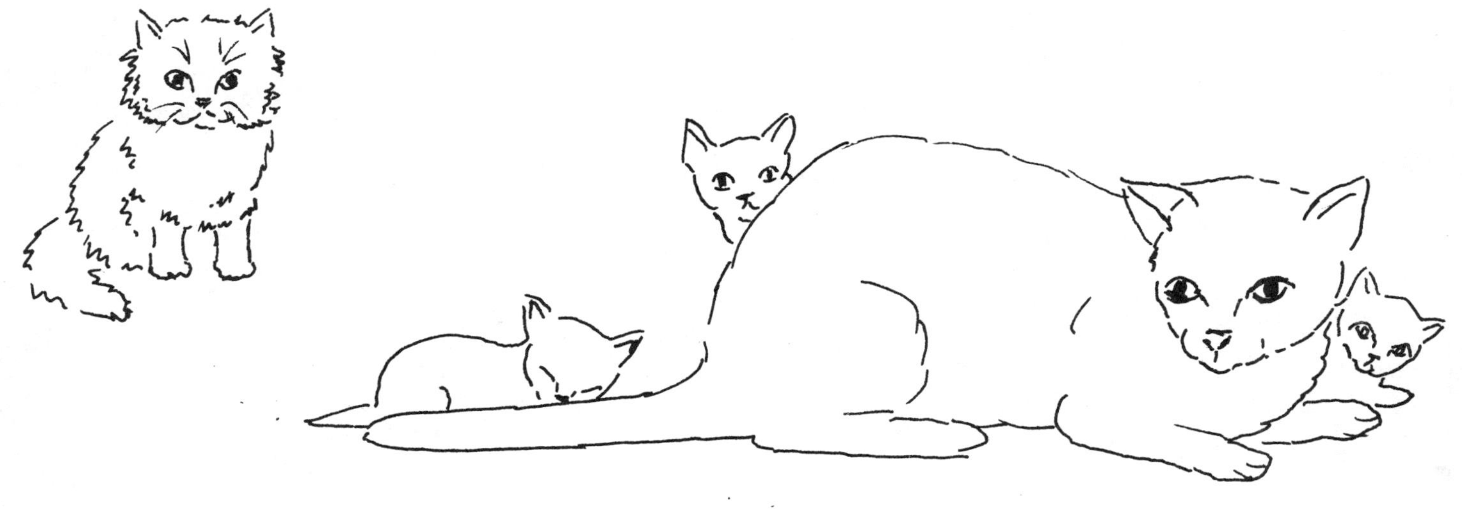

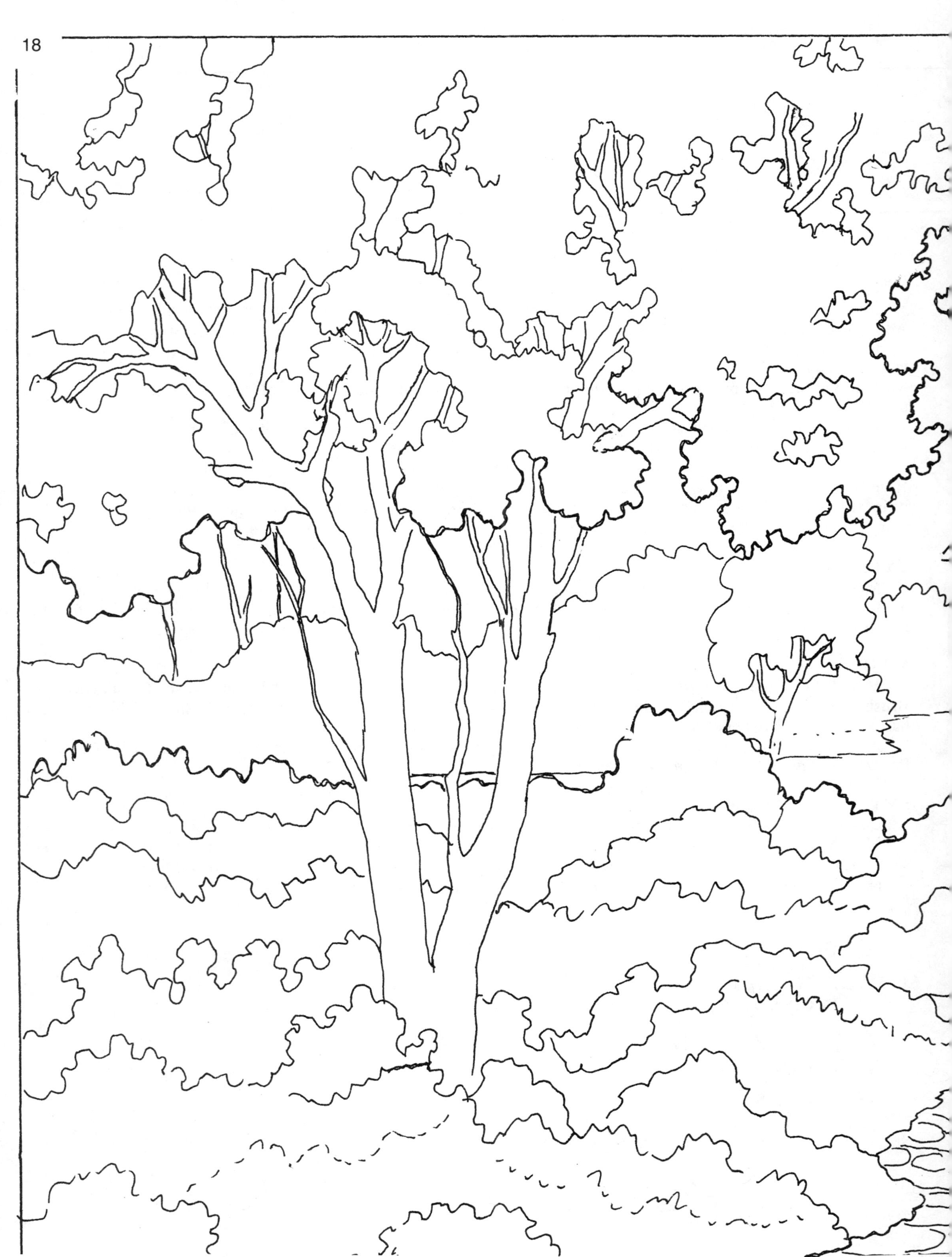

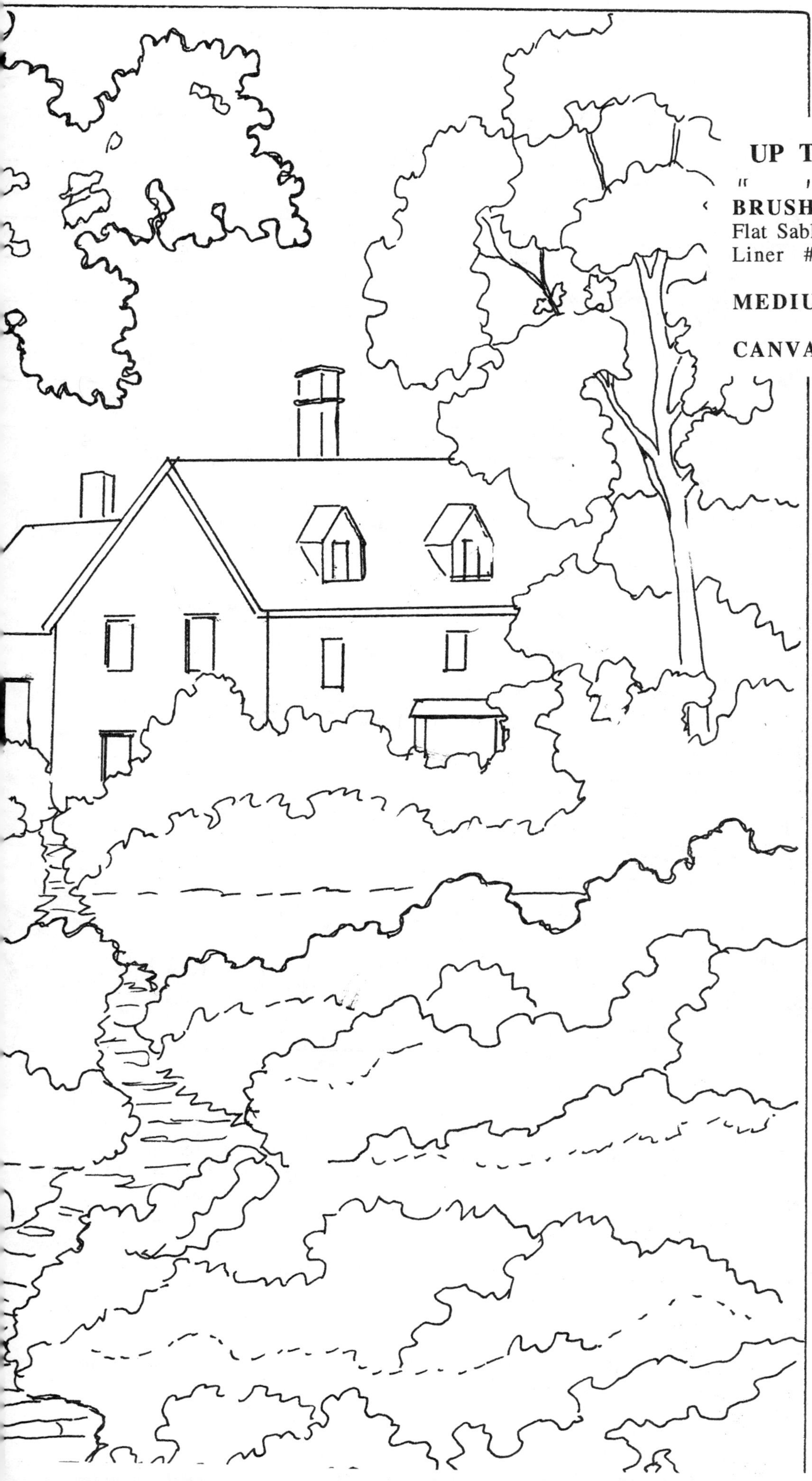

UP THE GARDEN PATH

BRUSHES
Flat Sables #28, 18, 16, 12, 4
Liner #2

MEDIUM Stand Oil Light or L.O.T.

CANVAS: 14 x 18

PALETTE
White
Ultramarine Blue
Alizarin Crimson
Cadmium Red Light
Sap Green
Raw Umber
Cadmium Yellow Light
Paynes Gray
Yellow Ochre

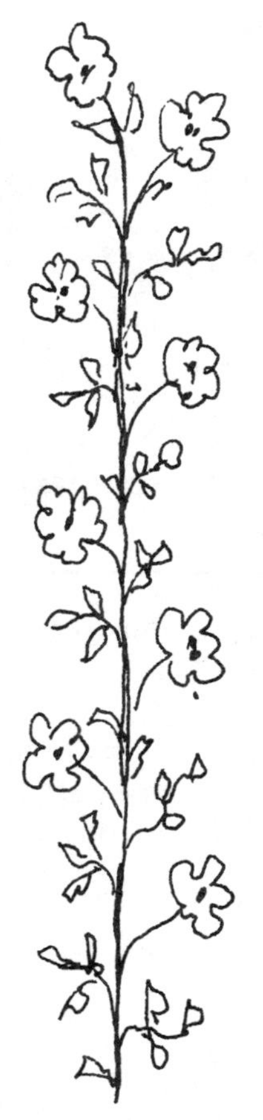

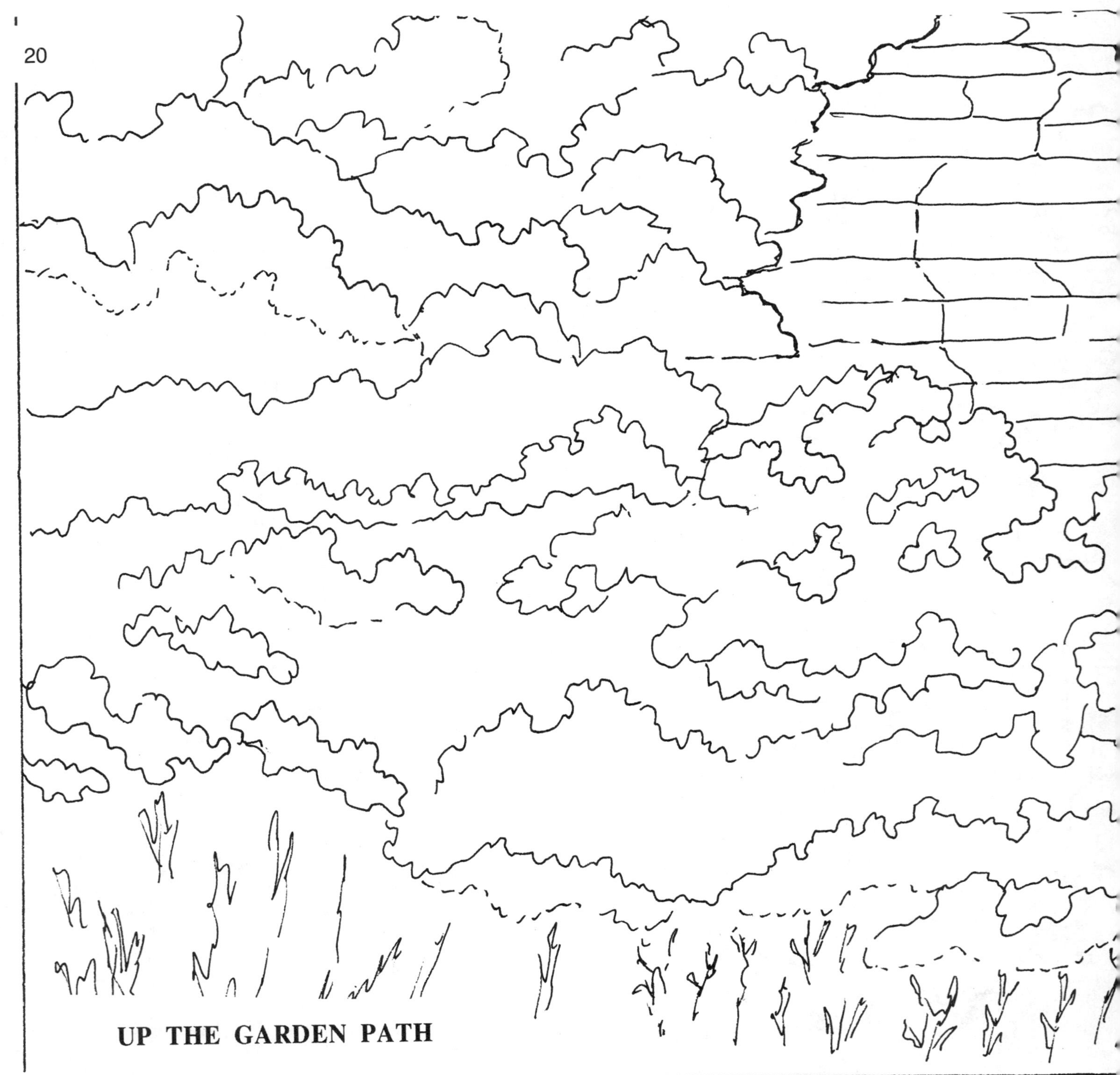

UP THE GARDEN PATH

Trace on the pattern

SKY

Mix Ultramarine Blue and White to make a light blue. Put in this color at the top of the sky and in the open spaces in the tree. Add more White to the sky above the house. Use a #28 flat sable and crisscross strokes. A little medium should be used.

ROOF

Mix Raw Umber, Paynes Gray and White to make a warm dark gray. Cover the roof using a #12 flat brush.

BRICK

Mix Cadmium Red Light, Yellow Ochre and White to make a dull orange for the brick. Apply with a #12 flat brush. Add a bit of Raw Umber to this color for the shadow side. Use dark gray for the windows. The edge of the #4 brush will be good for this step. Put in the trim with dirty brush using White.

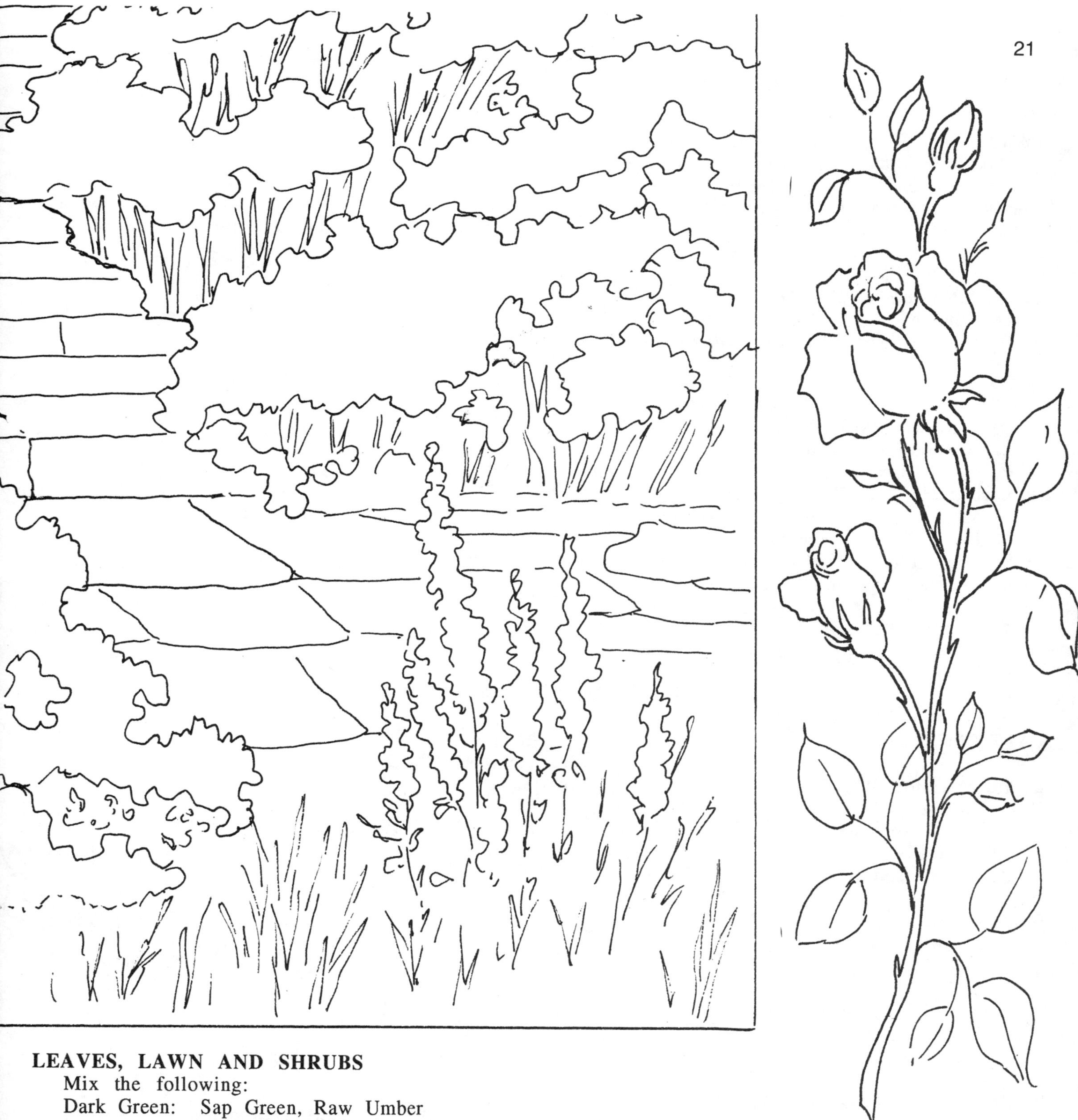

LEAVES, LAWN AND SHRUBS

Mix the following:
Dark Green: Sap Green, Raw Umber
Medium Green: Sap Green, Ultramarine Blue and White
Light Green: Sap Green, Cadmium Yellow Light, White

With a #18 flat brush dab in the background trees and bushes. Use medium green highlight with light green.

Cover the lawn with light green horizontal strokes using a #18 brush.

Use small amount of medium when absolutely necessary.

TREE TRUNK

Put in the tree trunk with dark gray. Highlight with the light brick color. Use vertical strokes with a #16 brush.

Add a bit of White to the dark gray for the small limbs. Use the edge of a #4 or a small liner. If you use a liner thin the paint with turpentine. Liners will not carry heavy paint.

UP THE GARDEN PATH

PATH
Mix Raw Umber and White to make a very light brown. Cover the path with this color using horizontal strokes with a #18 brush. Mix a bit of White in the dark gray to make medium gray. Use this for the details. Apply with a #16 brush. Mix Yellow Ochre and White in the light brown to make a light sunny color for the highlights. When the path is dry mix a little green each and medium to make shadows on the path.

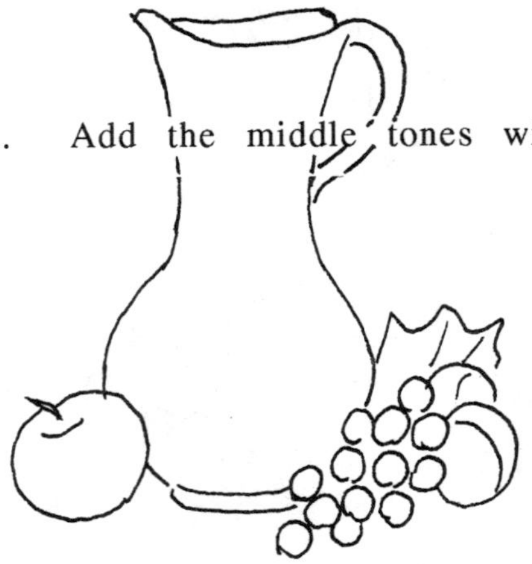

TREE LEAVES AND SHRUBS
Dab in the dark areas with dark green using a #18 brush. Add the middle tones with the medium green and highlight with light green.

FLOWERS
Mix the following flower colors:
Deep Rose : Alizarin Crimson
Light Rose: Add White to rose
Purple: Alizarin Crimson, Ultramarine Blue and White
Lavender: Add White to purple
Orange Add White to the brick color
Medium Blue: Ultramarine Blue and White
See the color illustration for different colors. Use the corner of a #16 brush to dab in these colors in the appropriate places.

STILL LIFE WITH PITCHER

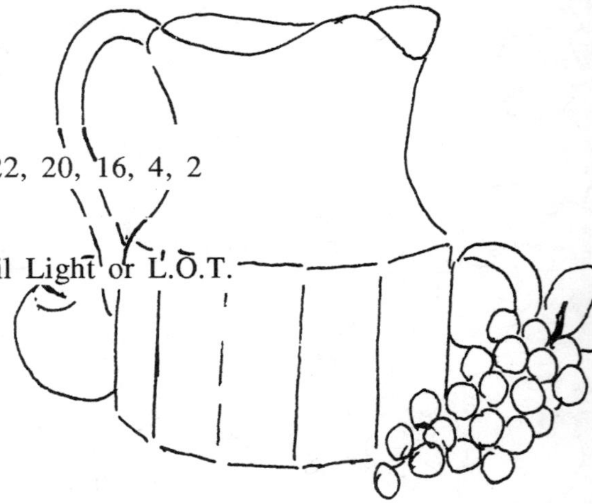

PALETTE
White
Brilliant Yellow Light
Mars Yellow
Cadmium Yellow Light
Ultramarine Blue
Alizarin Crimson
Grumbacher Red
Burnt Umber
Raw Sienna
Transparent Gold Ochre

BRUSHES
Flat Sables #32, 28, 22, 20, 16, 4, 2
Spotter #1

MEDIUM Stand Oil Light or L.O.T.

CANVAS: 12 x 16

Prime the canvas with turpentine tinted to a light tan with Raw Sienna. Allow this to dry. Trace on the pattern.
This picture is for detail lovers and is a picture to be worked several times.

BACKGROUND AND SHADOWS
Mix a deep brown color using Ultramarine Blue, Alizarin Crimson and Mars Yellow.
With a #32 flat sable brush fill in the background using crisscross strokes. Paint the shadow area under the table with this color.
Mix a little Brilliant Yellow Light with this color to lighten it. Crisscross some into the background to lighten it. Use some medium as necessary.

PITCHER
Cover the pitcher using Brilliant Yellow Light Tint this color with background color for the shadows or the side panels and handle. Use a #22 flat brush with crisscross strokes. A bit of medium may be needed. Highlight with White. Allow it to dry. Then glaze the pitcher with Transparent Gold Ochre. Mix with Stand Oil or L.O.T. to make a pale yellow. Brush it over the pitcher using a #28 flat. Add a dark line under the pitcher to "set" it down on the table.

You may want to repaint more than once. Sometimes the more you work a still life the better it gets.

After the pitcher is dry add the details with Ultramarine Blue and dull red.

Dull red is made from Grumbacher Red and a tiny bit of Burnt Umber. Use #4 and #2 flat brushes for this step.

Smooth the #2 to a knife edge for the tiny lines. You may use a #1 spotter if you are more comfortable with it. The lines on the real pitcher were not perfect. This is true of much of the old pottery.

FRUIT

GRAPES:

Mix Ultramarine Blue and Alizarin Crimson to make a deep purple. Paint the whole grape area with this color using a #22 flat to apply the base color.

Add White to the base color to make a lighter purple. Other shades are made by adding more Alizarin Crimson or Ultramarine Blue to this color.

Use a #16 brush to pick out the individual grape shapes.

Notice the pinker tones on the light sides and bluer shades as back lights. Use a #2 flat with White to do highlights. Work this into a small area. Then use a final dab of White for a shine.

PEARS:

Mars Yellow is the basic pear color. Paint with a #18 flat using crisscross strokes. Add some White to the light areas.

Use a #16 brush and dab or crisscross in bits of the shadow color. Add Grumbacher Red for the blush.

Mix a green from Ultramarine Blue and Cadmium Yellow. Gently dab some of this into the shadow areas. Stems are light brown shaded with dark brown.

APPLE:

Mix a deep red from Alizarin Crimson and Grumbacher Red. Use the pear colors for the stripes. Apply the paint with a #16 flat following the vertical roundness of the apple. Use a #4 flat for the highlight. Work in a small spot of White and use a final dab of White for a high shine. Use medium as necessary.

PEACHES:

Mix the following:

Medium Red: Grumbacher Red, Alizarin Crimson and White

Deep Yellow: Cadmium Yellow Light and Grumbacher Red

Deep Rose: Alizarin Crimson and White

Dull Red: Grumbacher Red and Burnt Umber

Use a #20 flat brush to cover the red side of the peaches. Cover the yellow areas and blend edge of the two colors on the back half of the peaches.

Crisscross a bit of yellow into the red side to lighten the middle area so that they will appear rounder. Use a tiny bit of dark brown (background color) along the crease.

TABLE

Use horizontal strokes with a #28 flat brush paint the table with Raw Sienna.

Mix a lighter shade by adding White and Mars Yellow. Streak the wood with this color, especially along the front edge.

Add dark streaks of shadow color to make wood grain. More shadow color will be needed on the front edge of the table. Use medium as necessary.

CLOTH

Cover the cloth area with White gradually fading into the dark background. Use a bit of medium.

Mix a little bit of Ultramarine Blue into the background color and add White to make a light gray. Use this color to put in the wrinkles. A #20 brush is right for this. Highlight with Brilliant Yellow Light.

With a #4 flat brush add the shadow under the edge of the cloth.

Use the light gray for the shadows of the grapes on the right.

Sign and enjoy.

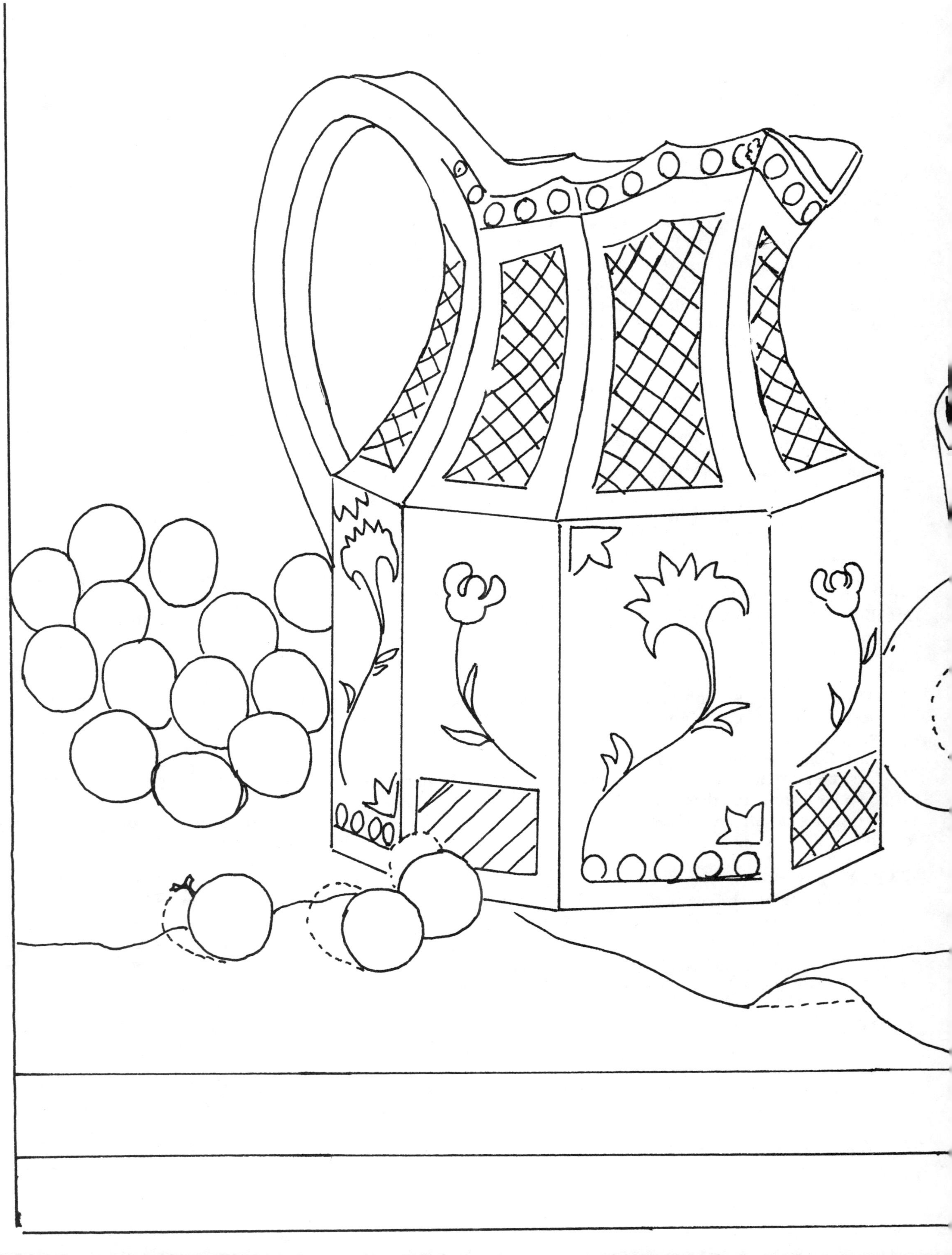

STILL LIFE WITH PITCHER

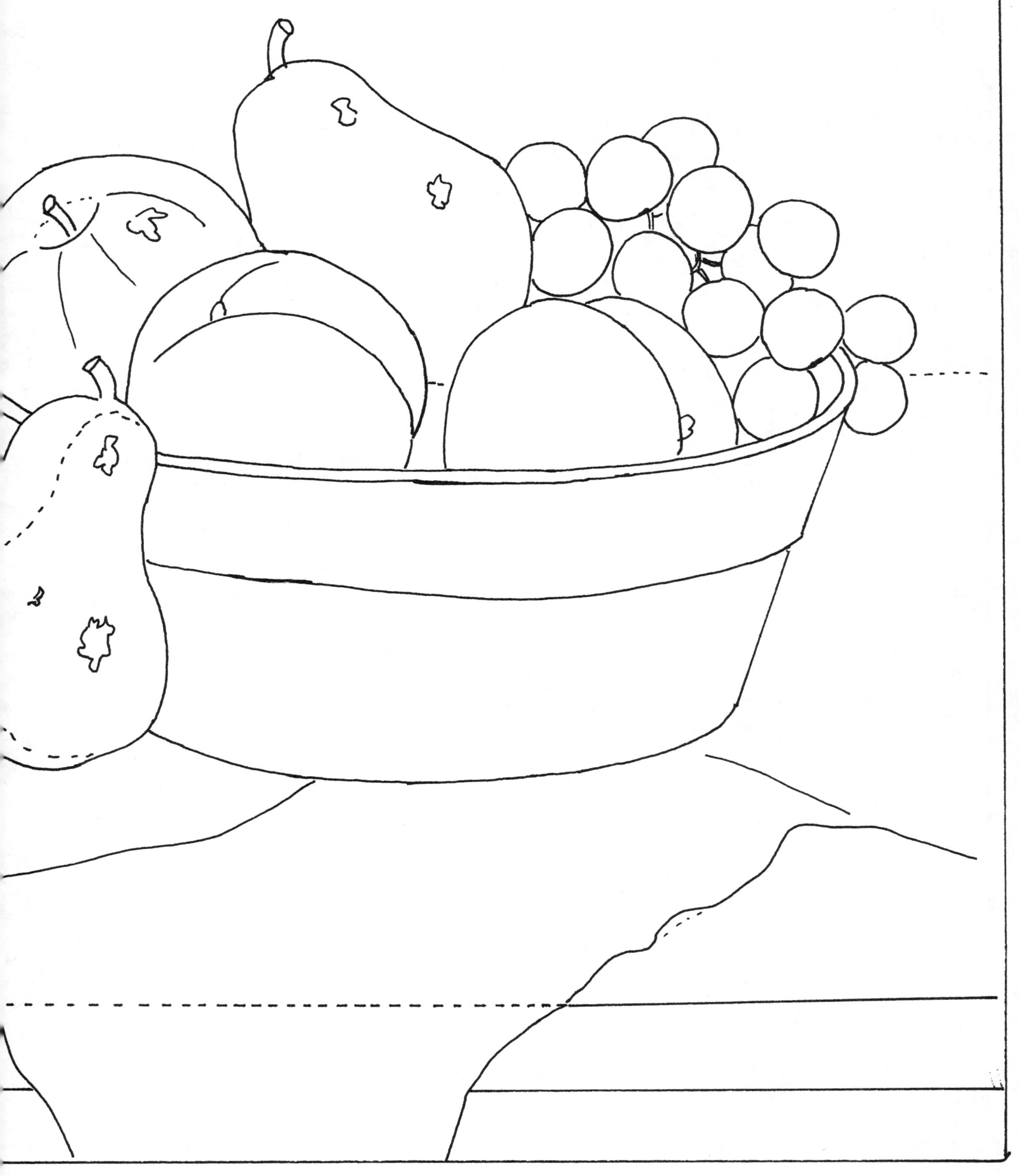

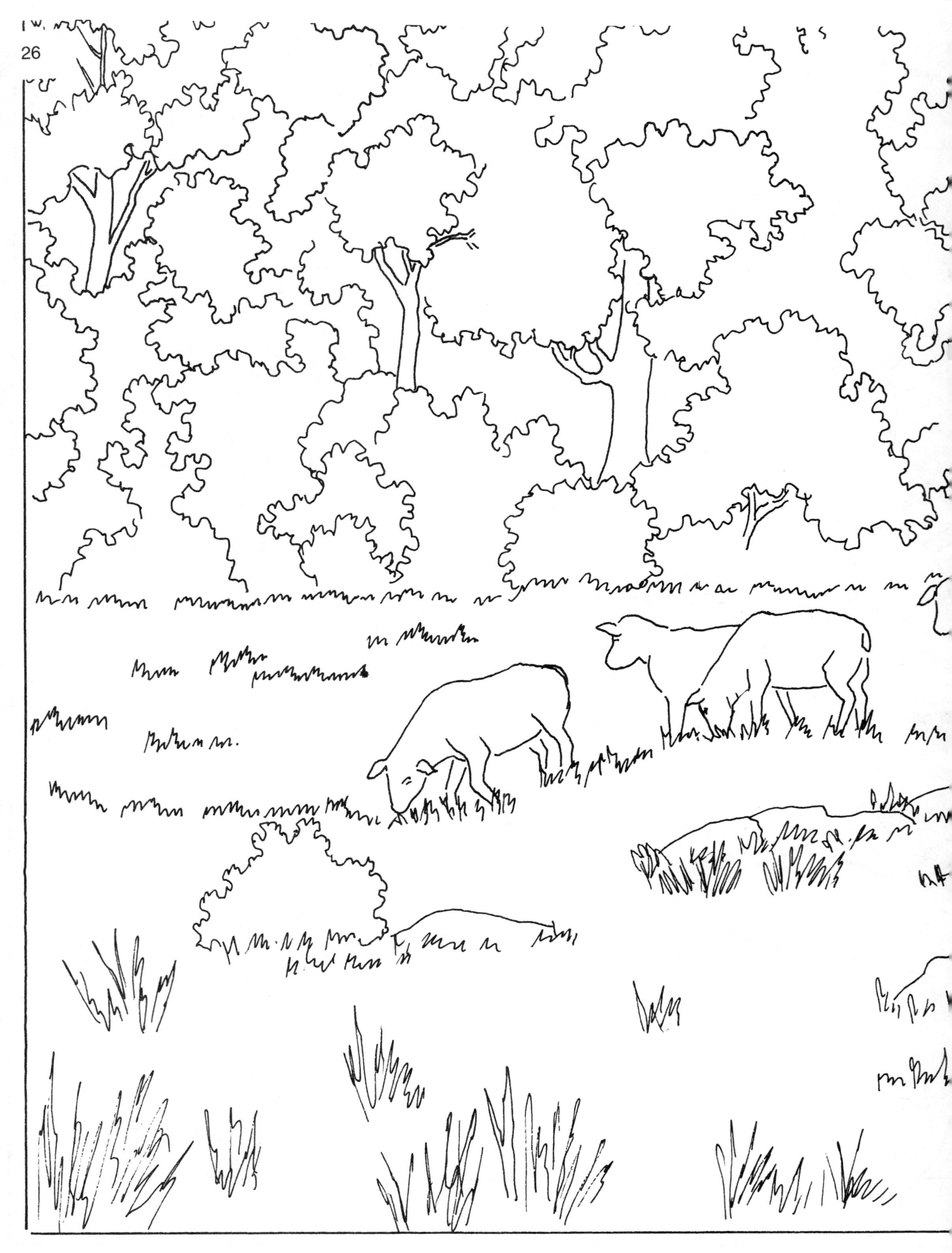

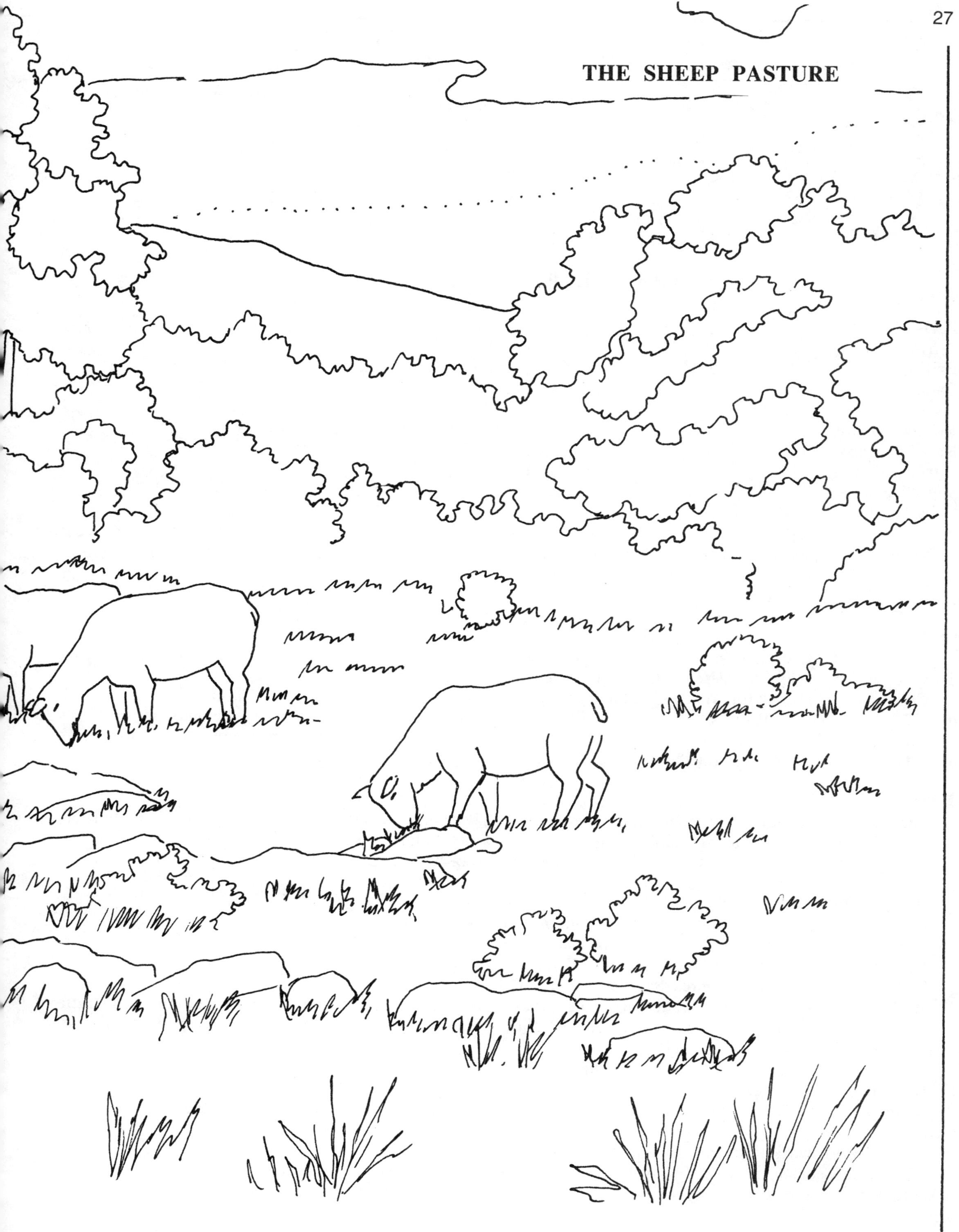
THE SHEEP PASTURE

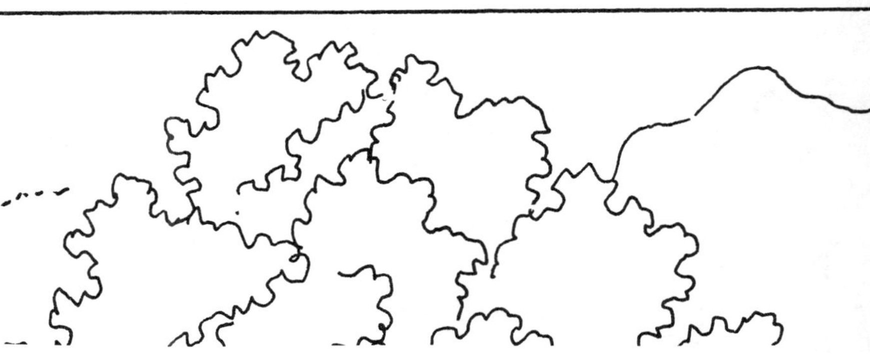

THE SHEEP PASTURE

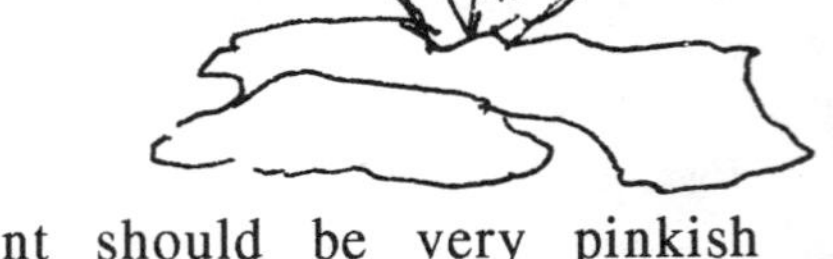

PALETTE
White
Brilliant Yellow Light (Permalba)
Cadmium Red Light
Cadmium Yellow Light
Yellow Ochre
Raw Sienna
Burnt Sienna
Sap Green
Cobalt Blue

BRUSHES
Flat Sables #28, 16, 12, 4, 2
Stippler #2
Fan Brush #2

MEDIUM Stand Oil Light or L.O.T.

CANVAS: 12 x 16

Prime the canvas with turpentine tinted with Burnt Sienna. The tint should be very pinkish tan. Allow to dry.

Trace on the pattern.

SKY

Mix Cobalt Blue and White to make light blue. With a #28 flat brush cove the light blue areas, using crisscross strokes. Use a tiny bit of medium when necessary.

Cover the clouds with White. Blend the edges into the blue areas. Use a circular motion with the #28 brush. A bit of Brilliant Yellow Light for highlights will brighten the clouds.

Add a little Cadmium Red Light to the blue sky color to make a medium mauve. Use this for the distant hill. Use the #18 flat brush and follow the contour of the land.

TREES

For the distant trees add some Sap Green and Raw Umber to the sky color to make a cool blue green. Cover the area using dabbing strokes with a #12 flat brush.

For the large middle ground trees mix the following colors

Dark Green: Sap Green and Raw Umber
Warm Brown: Burnt Sienna, Cadmium Red Light
Light Warm Brown: Raw Sienna, Cadmium Red Light and Yellow Ochre
Orange: Cadmium Red Light, Yellow Ochre
Dull Yellow: Yellow Ochre, Cadmium Yellow Light and White
Light Green: Yellow Ochre, Sap Green and White

With the #28 flat brush underpaint the trees using crisscross strokes. Look at the illustration for the colors behind the middle tones and lights. The trees are numbered on the pattern for your convenience.

From left to right, tree #1 has a dark green background. Trees #3 and #4 have light warm brown underpainting.

Cover the remaining bush and tree areas with the above colors as you see them in the color illustration.

Continue to work the trees while the underpaint is wet.

Add a few dabs of warm brown to tree #1. Then use the light green for highlights. Dab in these colors with a #16 brush or with a #2 stippler. You should use the brush that works best for you.

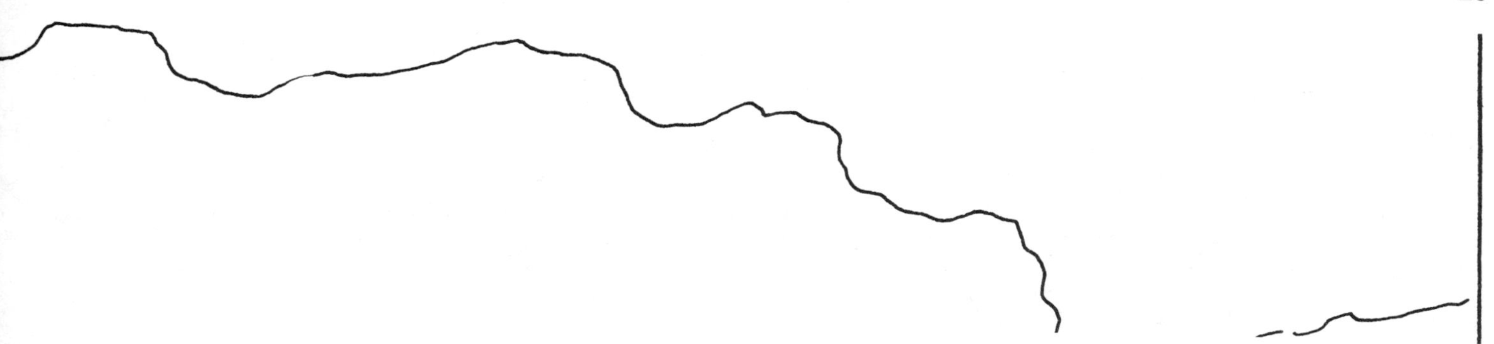

The middle tones on tree #2 are done with orange on the left side and light brown on the shadow side. Add highlights with orange lightened with White or Cadmium Yellow Light.

Use Cadmium Yellow Light and orange on tree #3 and dull yellow on tree #4. Dab the light color over the wet underpainting. Allow underpainting to show through for shadow places.

Highlight with middle tone colors lifted with a little White.

Put in the tree trunks with a #2 or #4 flat brush. Use Raw Umber softened with White for the dark ones and White softened with Raw Umber for the light one.

GROUND

With a #28 brush apply the paint using horizontal strokes. Use the tree colors starting with the lightest shades (dull yellow and light green) near the tree line.

As you move toward the bottom of the canvas the colors will become darker and richer.

Omit the brightest colors on the ground work.

Add some White to the light colors for a higher lift. Pat a little on for grass tips behind the sheep. Use a #2 fan brush.

SHEEP

Mix a dull medium gray from Raw Umber, Cobalt Blue and White. Use a #2 or 4 brush to put in the darks on the sheep. Use White softened with the dull gray for the light areas. Highlight with Brilliant Yellow Light.

Use a #2 fan brush to pat in the grass using a lighter color than the background color.

ROCKS

Mix Raw Umber and White to make a medium brown. With a #16 brush put in the dark areas of the rocks. Add more White to this mix for the light areas. It is good if you pick up a little green from the grass occasionally.

GRASS AND BUSHES

Moving toward the bottom of the canvas use the edge of a #12 flat brush to make vertical strokes for a grassy look.

Form horizontal lines of light and dark grasses. This makes the ground look flat. Don't get too obvious with the horizontal lines.

Dab in a few bushes with the corner of the #16 brush. Use the tree colors as you will.

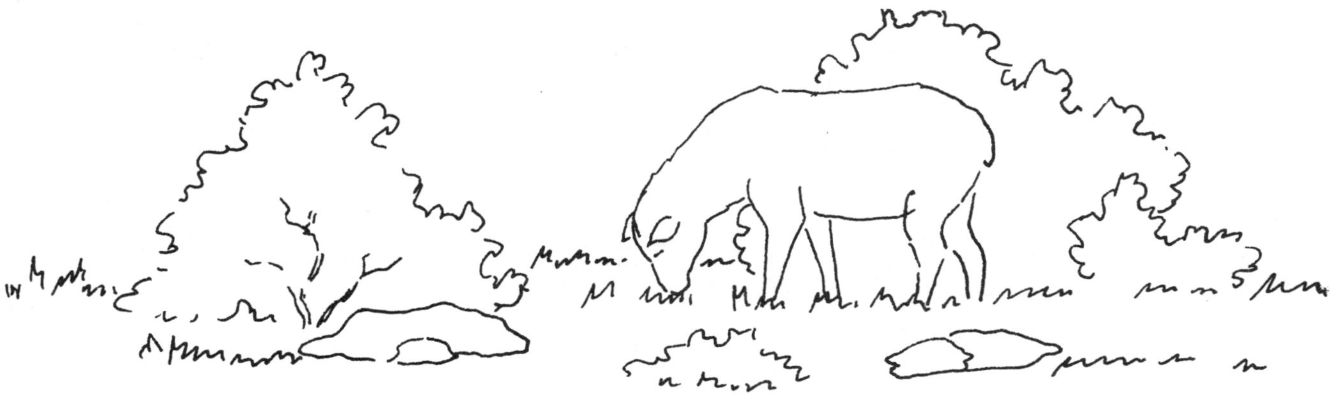

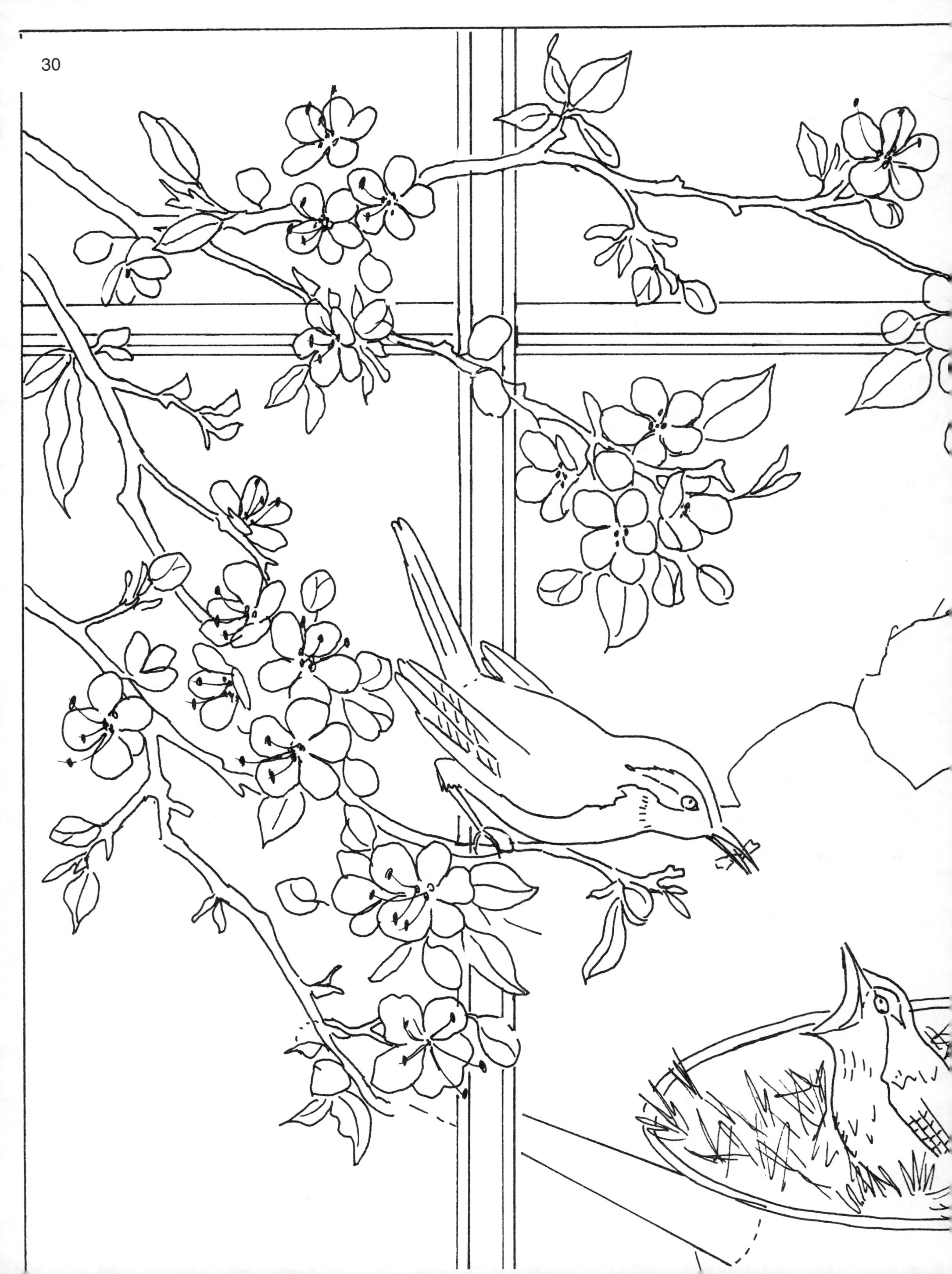

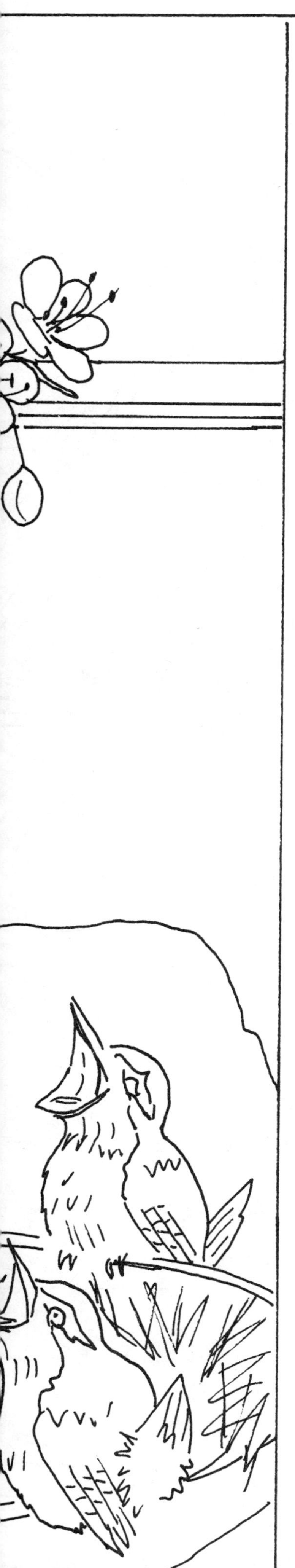

WRENS

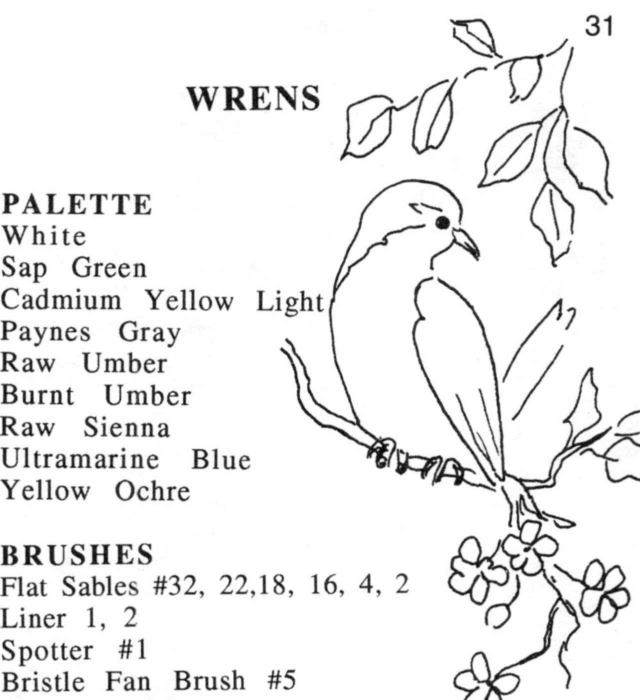

PALETTE
White
Sap Green
Cadmium Yellow Light
Paynes Gray
Raw Umber
Burnt Umber
Raw Sienna
Ultramarine Blue
Yellow Ochre

BRUSHES
Flat Sables #32, 22,18, 16, 4, 2
Liner 1, 2
Spotter #1
Bristle Fan Brush #5
18 Inch Ruler

MEDIUM: Stand Oil Light or L.O.T.
Turpentine
CANVAS: 14 x 18

Prime the canvas with turpentine tinted with Burnt Sienna. Allow this to dry.

Trace the pattern on the canvas, except the branch and flowers.

WINDOW PANES

Mix the following:

Dark Gray: Paynes Gray, Raw Umber, White

Medium Blue: Ultramarine Blue, Raw Umber and White

Light Blue: Ultramarine Blue, Paynes and White

Tan: Raw Sienna and White

Light Green: Sap Green, Cadmium Yellow Light and White

Brown: Raw Umber, Paynes Gray and White

With a #32 brush crisscross in these colors in the appropriate places. See the color illustration for this. Some medium will be necessary.

Cover the area inside the broken pane with brown and dark gray.

Use the same brush and method.

The glass in front of the pan is done with medium blue. Add fine White lines for cracks in the glass using a #1 liner or #1 spotter.

PAN

Add Paynes Gray to Ultramarine Blue to make a really dark blue. Paint the darkest parts of the pan

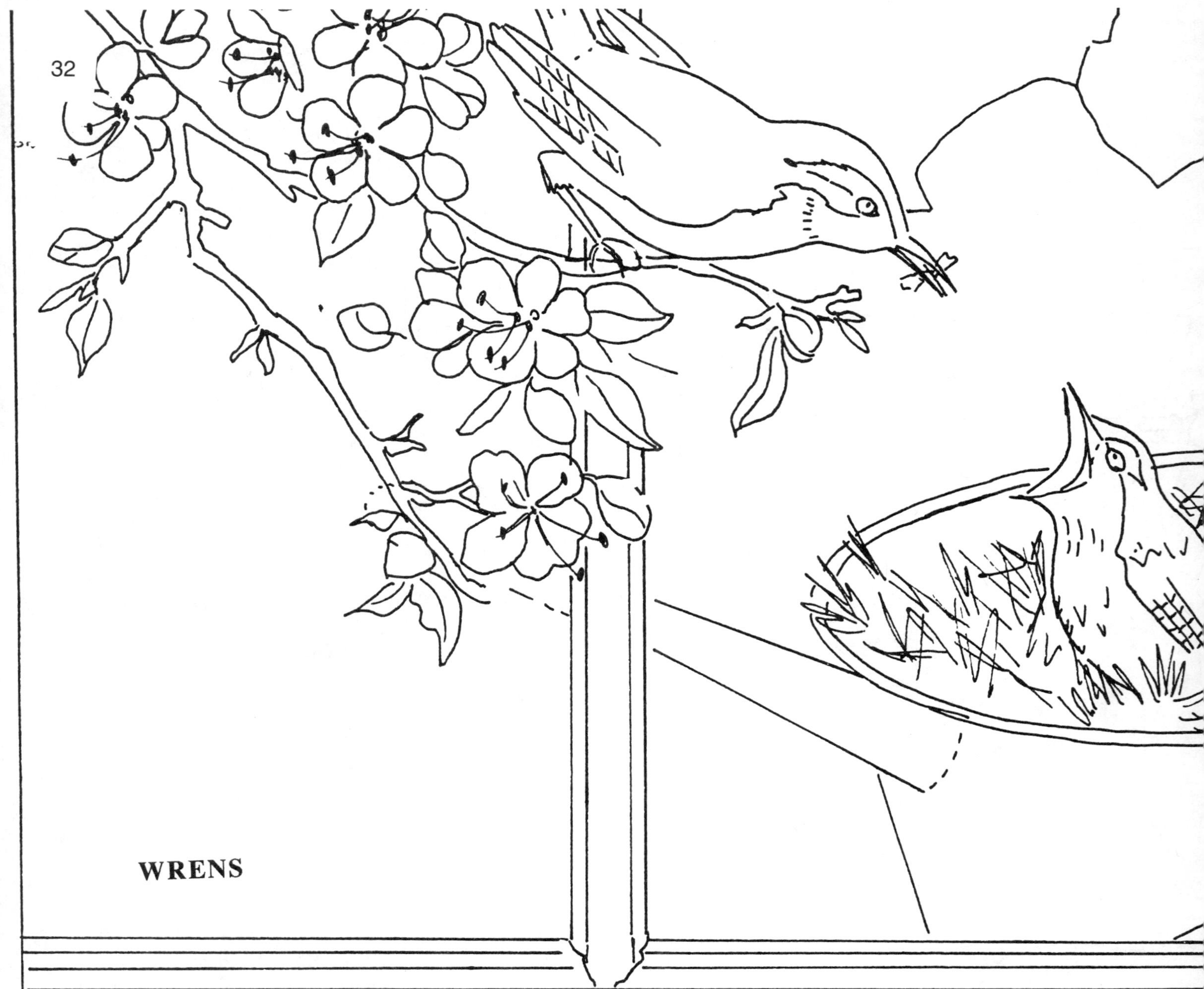

STRAW NEST

Use previously mixed colors for the straw. A dark background with light straw over it will do. Use a #2 liner for this. When using a liner, thin the paint with turpentine.

BRANCH AND FLOWERS

After everything is dry trace on the pattern for the branch and flowers.

Mix the following:

Deep Rose: Alizarine Crimson and White

Light Pink: Add more White to rose

Deep Green: Sap Green, Ultramarine Blue, White

Light Green: Sap Green, Cadmium Yellow Light and White

Put in the branches using Burnt Umber. Add the highlights with rust (from the birds). Use a #4 and a #2 flat for this.

FLOWERS

Use a #16 flat brush for the flowers. Light pink is the basic color. Pull the strokes toward the center. With a #4 flat brush add streaks of deep rose fanning out from the centers.

Add fine red lines with a #1 liner and a dot of yellow or pollen.

GREEN LEAVES

Cover the basic leaf with dark green. Use a #16 flat brush. Add the light green for highlights. Check the color illustration for places. Sign and enjoy.

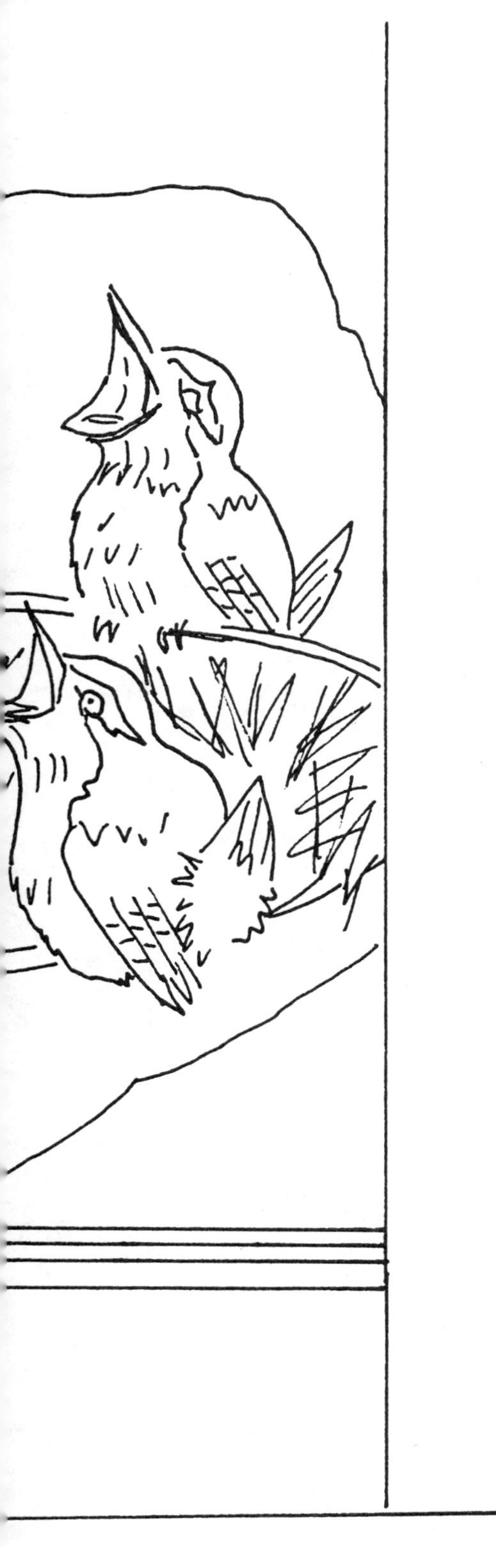

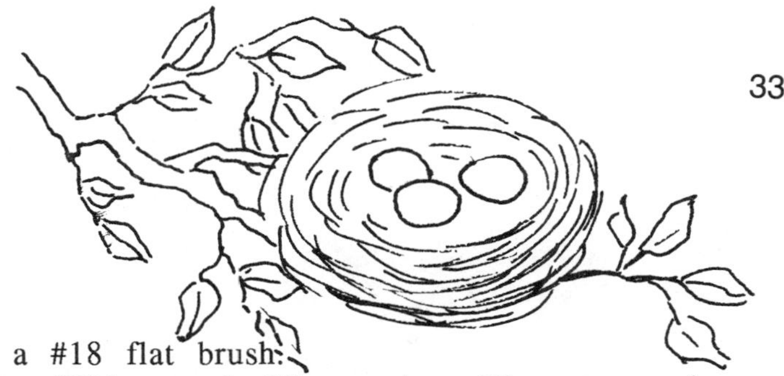

using a #18 flat brush.

Mix White and Ultramarine Blue to make a medium blue. Crisscross this into the rest of the pan. Use a #22 flat brush.

Work some White into the lightest areas of the pan. Add a light blue rim and edge to the handle.

Cover the window around the pan with paper and splatter the pan with White.

Thin some White with turpentine to make a liquid paint. Use a stiff brush such as a fan brush or a tooth brush.

Run your thumb over the bristles to make splatters. Practice on paper first.

WINDOW

Use the same colors that were mixed for the glass.

Add White to the dark gray to make a medium gray. With a #32 flat brush use strokes that follow the grain of the wood.

A ruler will be necessary to keep the lines straight.

Over the light gray base coat add dark gray for the cracks and shadows. Use the edge of a #18 or #16 flat brush. Add streaks of the other glass colors to make the wood grain. Use medium sparingly.

BIRDS

Mix the following colors:

Rust: Burnt Sienna, Cadmium Yellow Light and White

Dirty White: White, Paynes Gray, Raw Umber

Tan: Raw Sienna, White

Use a #16 or a #12 flat brush to cover the basic birds with rust on the back and dirty white on the breast. The strokes should move in the direction the feather would lay. Add Burnt Umber on the mother's wings.

On the mother bird add some light gray on the face and a bit of tan on her neck. After they are dry add the details.

Use Payne Gray for the little birds eyes and other dark trim. The eyes have a White dot for highlights. Add some White on the breast for highlights.

Use a #2 flat and a #1 spotter for the small parts.

Mix Alizarine Crimson and Cadmium Yellow Light and White to make a dark red for the babies throats. Add a yellow outline to their mouths. Use a #2 flat brush.

To the bird watchers, my apologies for the artistic license I took with the birds. There are so many kinds of wrens and these are somewhat generic.

PINK ROSES

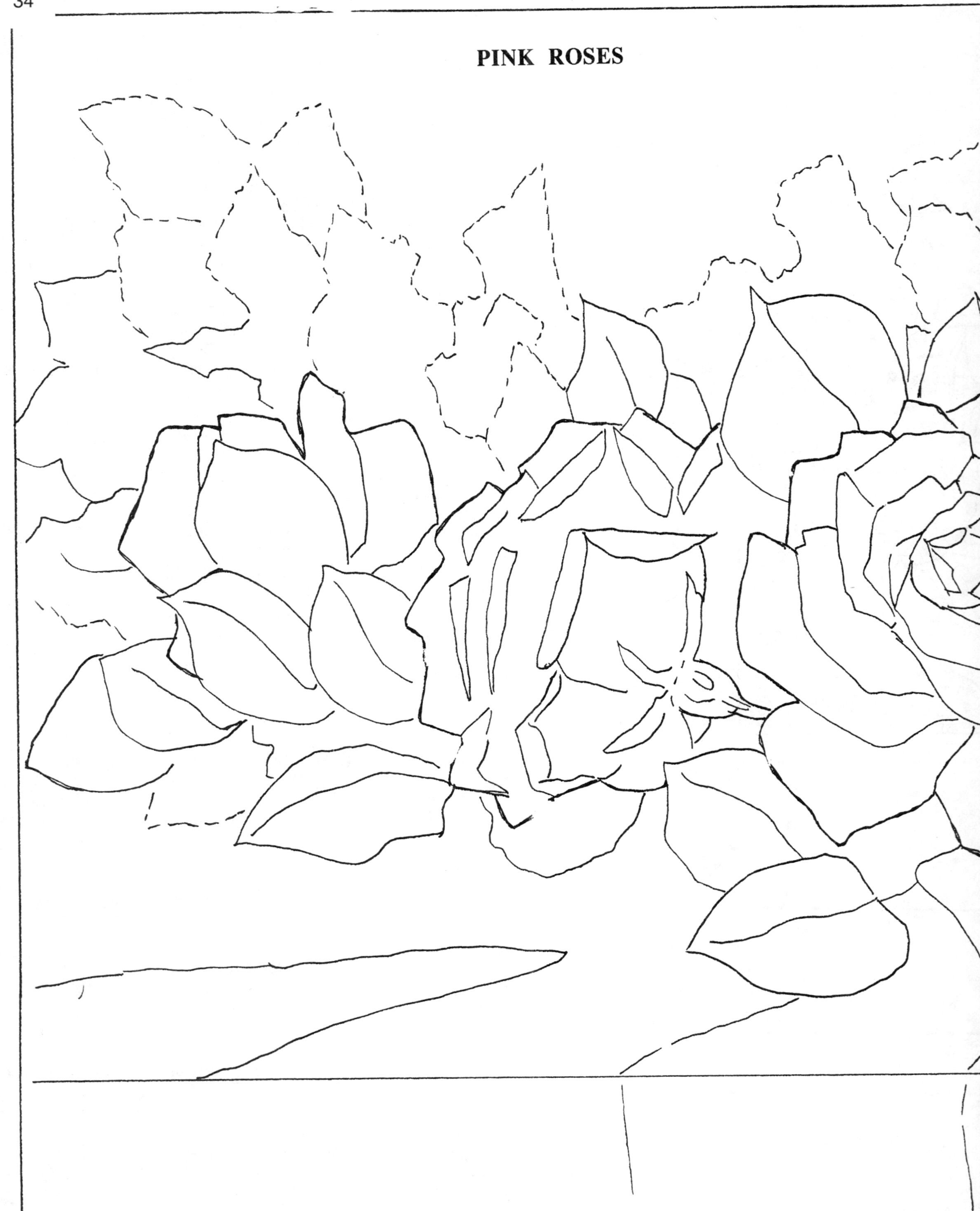

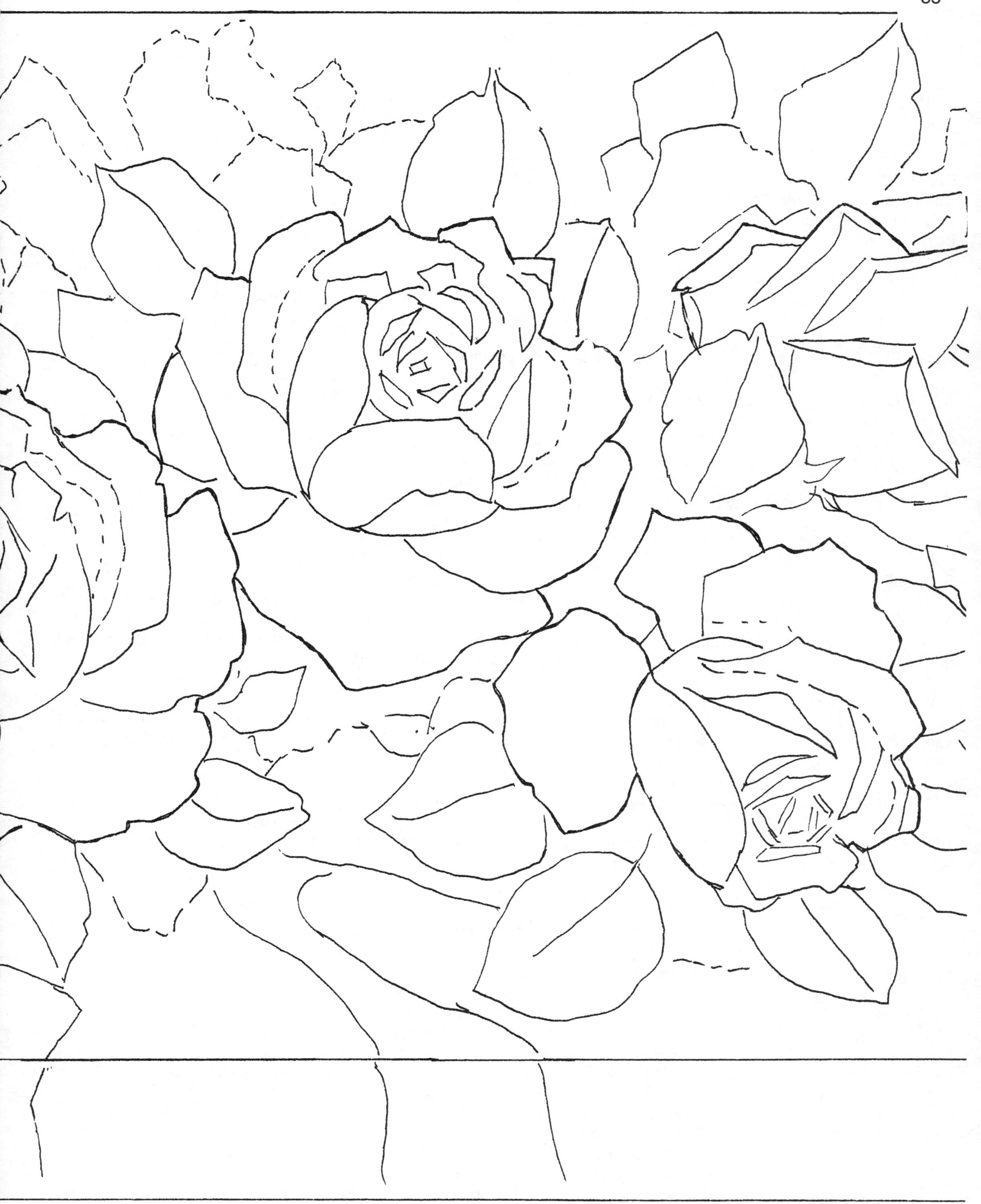

PINK ROSES

PALETTE
Titanium White
Brilliant Yellow Light
Cadmium Yellow Light
Thalo Yellow Green
Sap Green
Raw Umber
Cobalt Blue
Cadmium Red Light
Alizarin Crimson
Paynes Gray

BRUSHES
Flat Sables #44 (1 inch), 32,30,28 and 16

MEDIUM Stand Oil Light or L.O.T
Turpentine

CANVAS: 10 x 20

Trace on the pattern.

Prime the area of the roses with turpentine tinted with Thalo Yellow Green.

Prime the area around the roses with turpentine tinted with Sap Green and Raw Umber to make a greenish brown. Do not use much pigment in the turpentine. This will partially dry while you are doing the background. Use a one inch brush.

BACKGROUND AND TABLE CLOTH MIXES

Mix the following:

Medium Warm Gray: Raw Umber, Paynes Gray, a tiny bit of Alizarin Crimson and White.
Light Warm Gray: Add White to the medium warm gray.
Medium Gray: Raw Umber, Paynes Gray and White
Light Gray: Add White to the medium gray
Medium Cool Gray: Raw Umber, Paynes Gray, Sap Green, White
Dark Blue Gray: Paynes Gray, Cobalt Blue and a little White

BACKGROUND

Apply appropriate colors to the different areas. Start with the medium colors. Use a 1 inch flat brush. Cover the shadow leaves as indicated by the dotted lines on the pattern.

Load your brush with White. Use some medium to create a soft white. With the flat cut out the edges of the leaves. Gently brush the outer edges of the strokes into the background.

TABLE CLOTH

Use the colors of the background. First establish a table edge by drawing a line with a yardstick. Turpentine tinted with Paynes Gray will be right for this line. This line becomes a guide for the light and dark areas that form the edge.

PINK ROSES

Mix the following:

Deep Rose: Alizarin Crimson, Raw Umber (tiny bit) and White.
Medium Rose: Add White to the deep rose
Light Rose: Add more White
Pale Pink: Cadmium Red Light and White
Light Gray: Paynes Gray, Cobalt Blue and White

For the two roses on the left use medium rose for the background color. Add deep rose in the areas of deep shadow. Use a 1 inch flat brush. Some light grays will push back the edges.

The prominent petals are formed with deep rose on the far left flower. The next flower has petals made with light rose. Use a #28 brush and some medium as needed.

Apply some deep rose for the base of the roses on the right side. A bit of deep blue gray will bush back the edges. The base coat should be spread thin. Use medium very sparingly. You may use more medium in top layers of paint. The front petals are made with medium rose. Always apply details over wet paint in order to get a soft look.

For the three center roses use medium rose in the dark areas. A one inch flat brush will be best. Light rose is the color for the middle tone.

Allow a little of the Thalo Yellow Green wash to show through the rose colors.

If you lose this color you can put it back by adding White to Thalo Yellow Green and dabbing it in the center and base of the rose. Use the #16 brush for this. Notice the bits of almost pure red in the centers. This is for dramatic emphasis.

Add some light gray to the back edges to produce distance.

For the light petal areas you will probably be more comfortable with a #28 flat. Use the pale pink.

Highlight with some Brilliant Yellow Light. Use Permalba brand which is a warm white. Most other brands are too yellow for this step.

It is possible to use pure white for the highlights. This would produce cooler roses.

LEAVES

Mix the following

Deep Cool Green: Sap Green, Cobalt Blue and White

Light Cool Green: Add more White

Dark Warm Green: Sap Green with a tiny bit of Cadmium Red Light and White

Light Green: Sap Green, Cadmium Yellow Light and White

Use a #28 flat brush Put in the dark colors first. Check the color print for warm and cool areas.

Add the light greens while the base coat is wet.

When making leaves your strokes should swing toward the center vein. As you add highlights many of the strokes are pulled out from the center line using the flat of the brush.

Touches of Alizarin Crimson may be added for accent around the roses. Add a bit of light red on the edge of some leaves.

Mix some Sap Green, light red and White to make a greenish brown. Use this dark color for shadows under leaf edges.

Sign and enjoy.

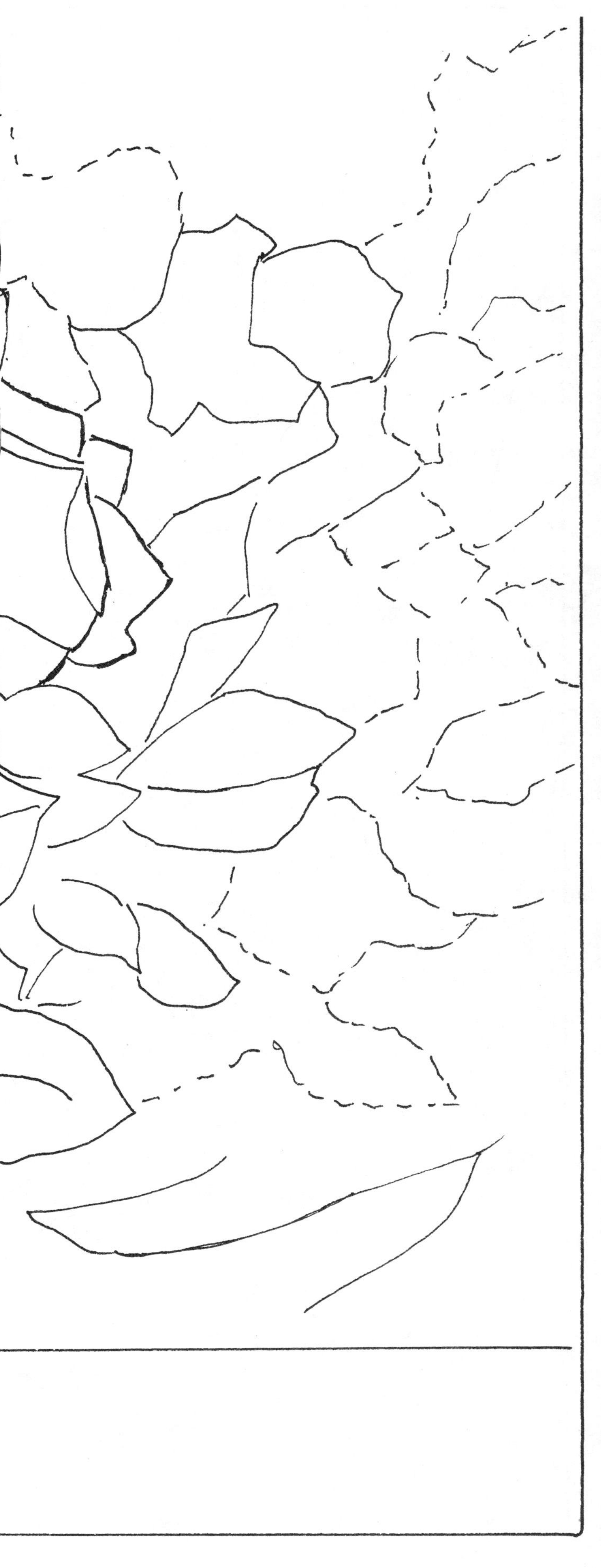

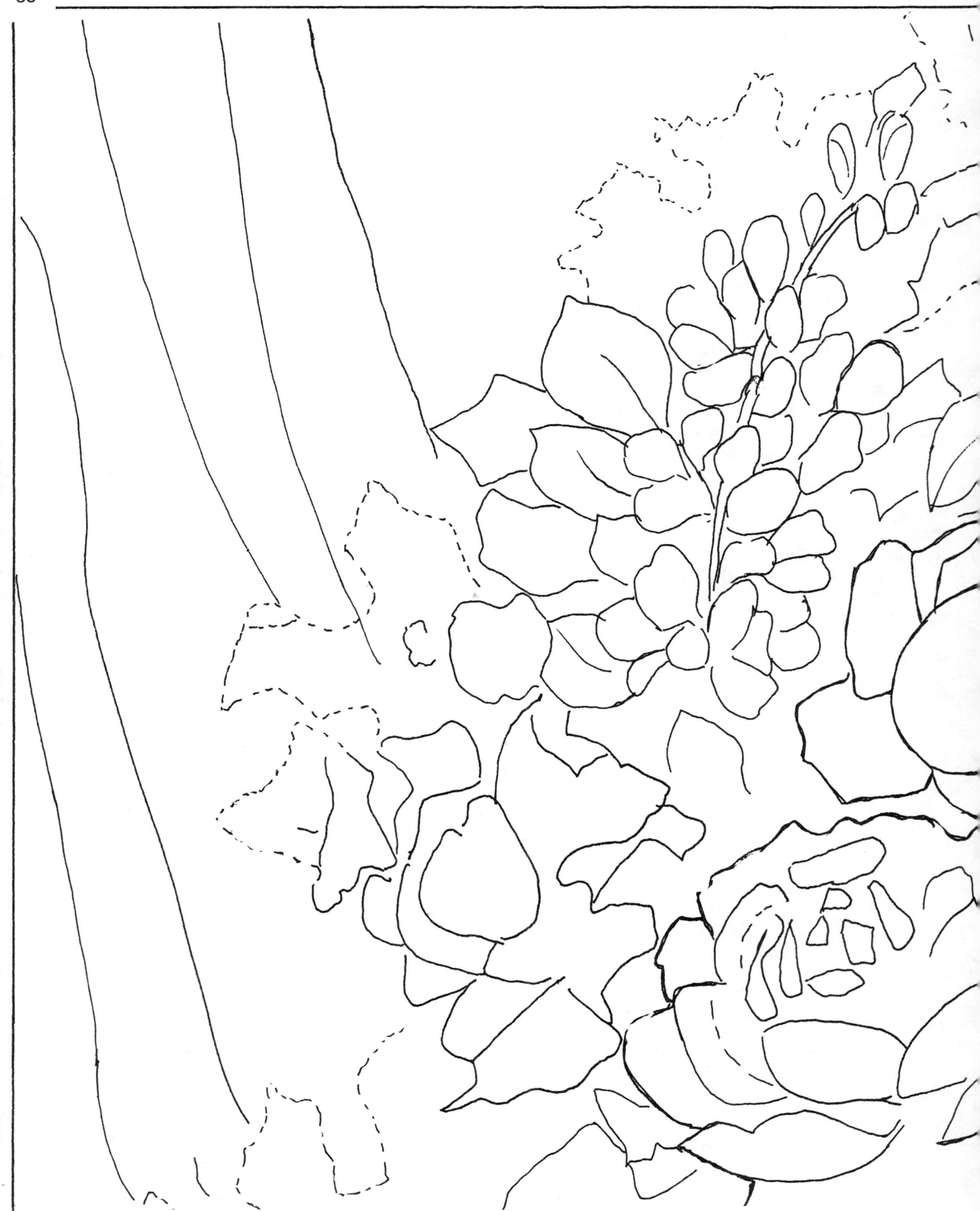

WHITE ROSES

PALETTE
White
Brilliant Yellow Light (Permalba)
Thalo Yellow Green
Cadmium Yellow Light
Cadmium Red Light
Alizarin Crimson
Sap Green
Cobalt Blue
Yellow Ochre

BRUSHES
Flat Sables #32, 22, 18

MEDIUM Stand Oil Light or L.O.T.
Turpentine

CANVAS: 16 x 20

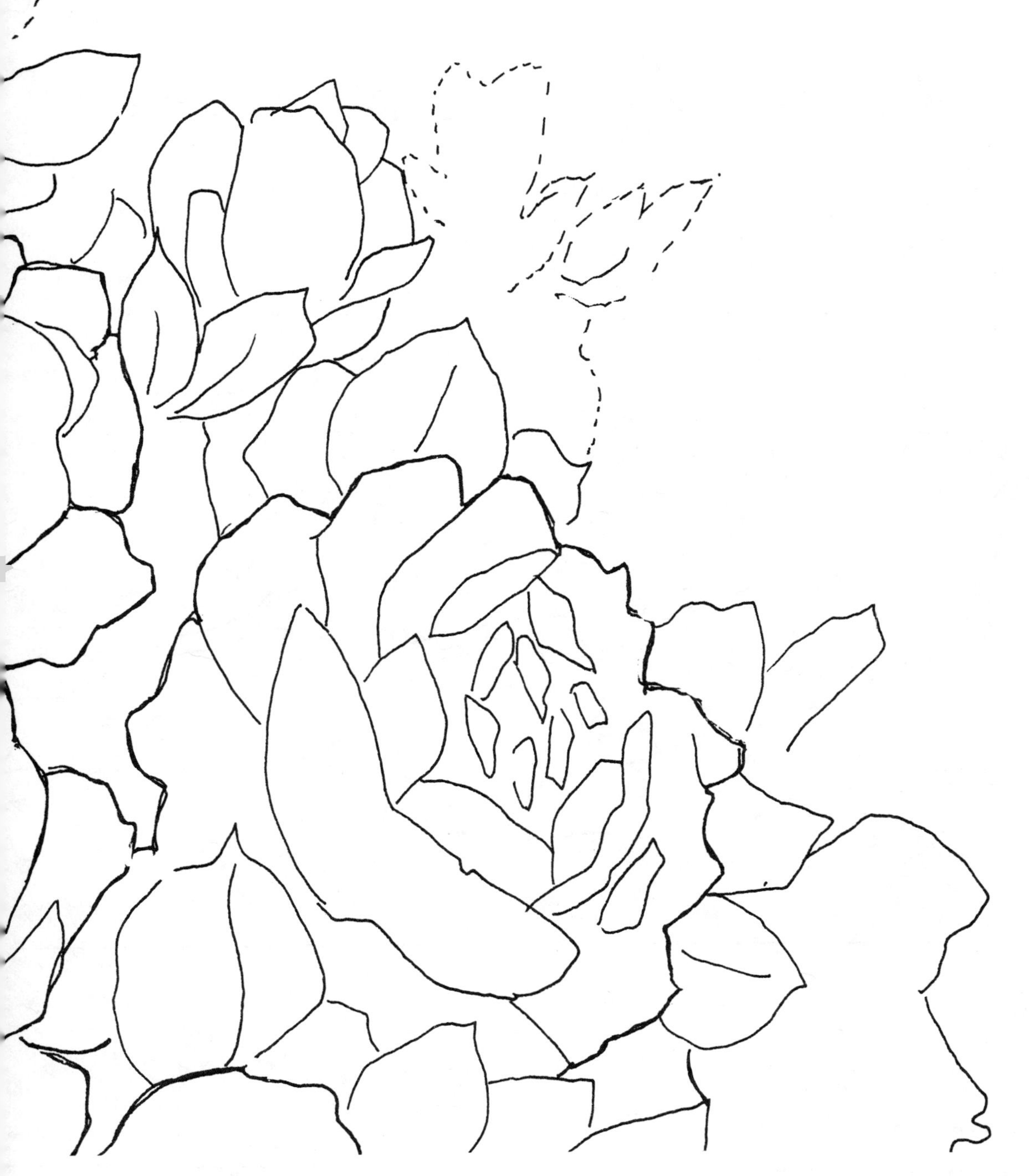

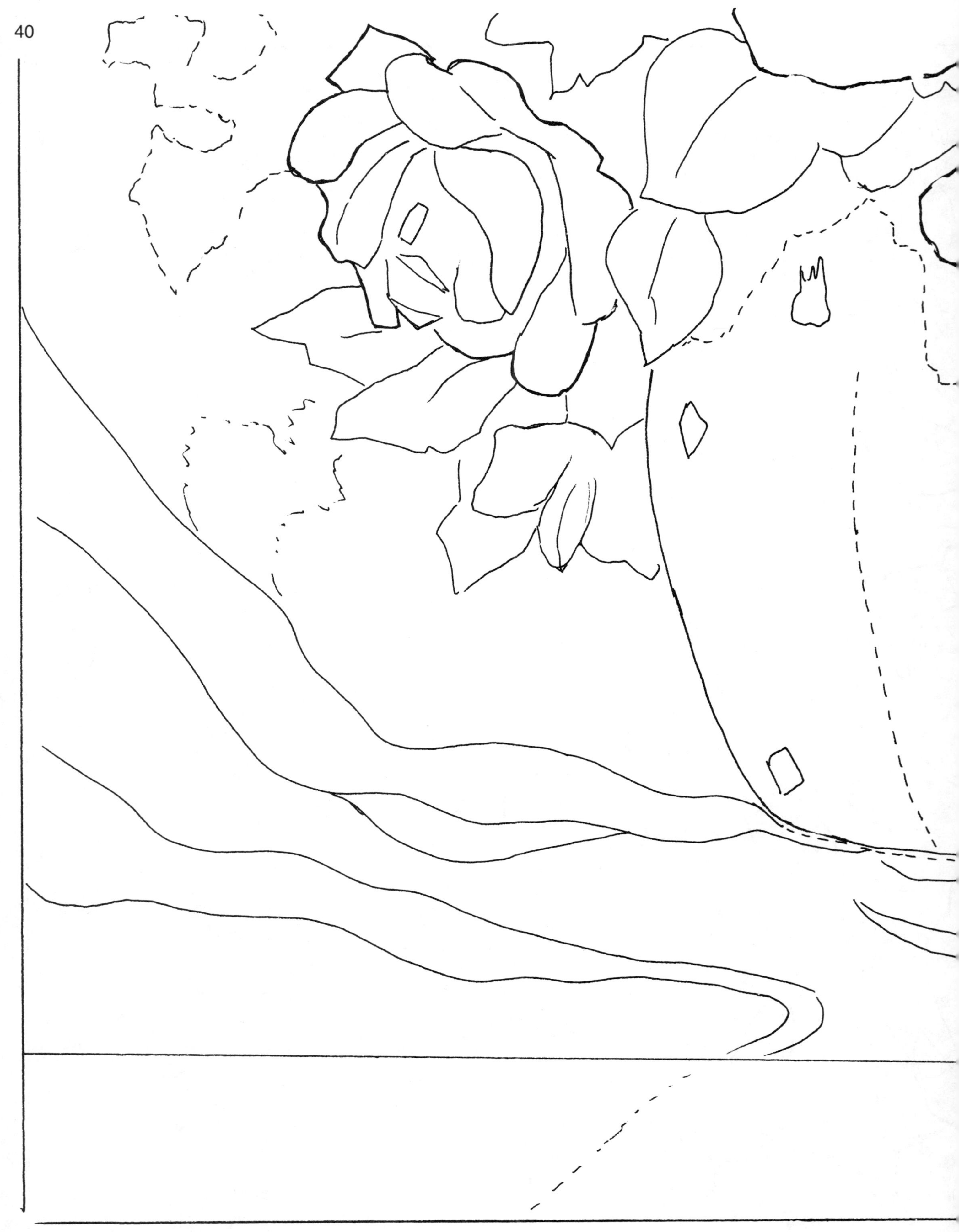

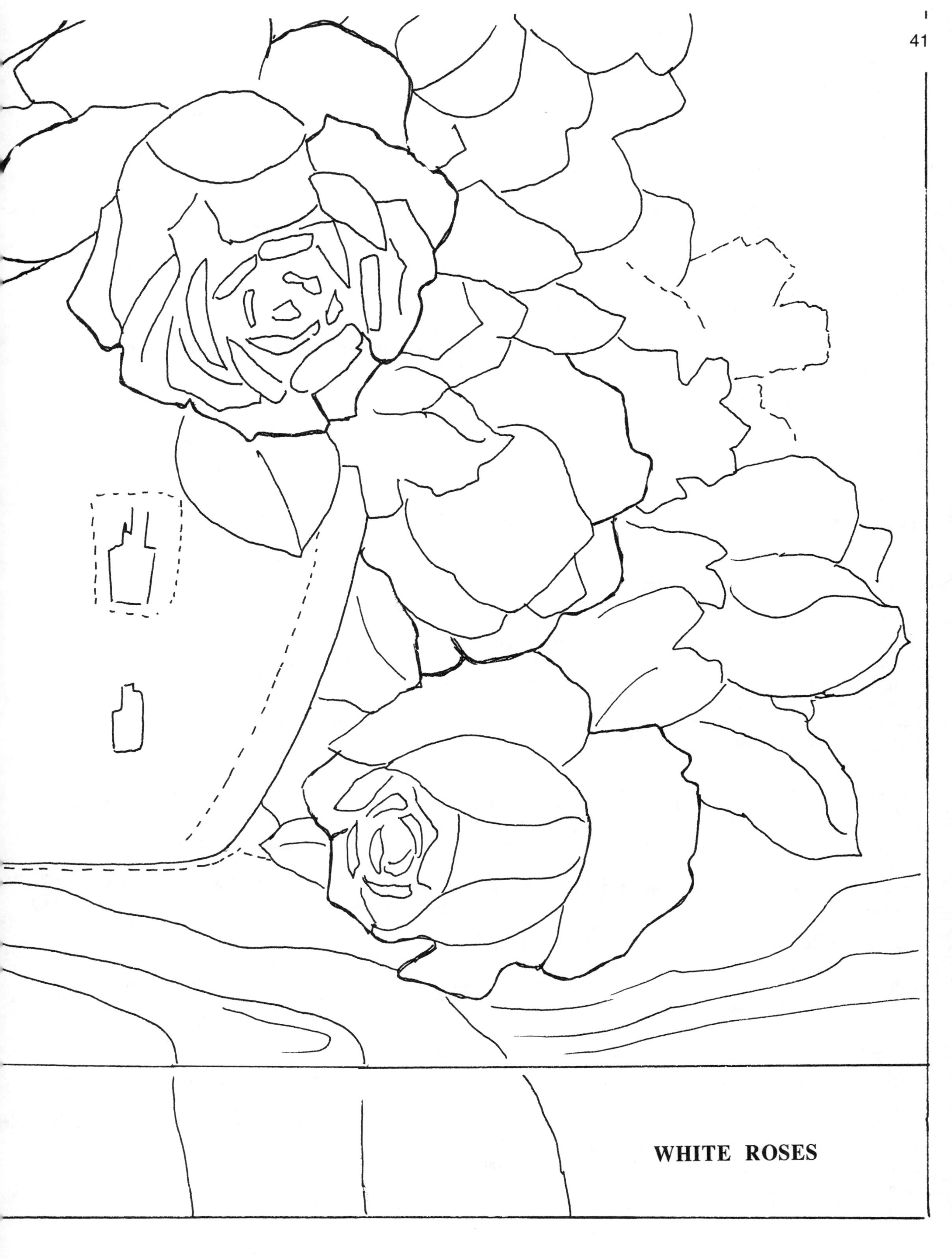
WHITE ROSES

WHITE ROSES

Trace the pattern on the canvas.

Prime the canvas in the flower area using turpentine tinted to a light green with Thalo Yellow Green

Mix the following colors:

Dark Warm Gray: Cobalt Blue, Cadmium Red Light, Yellow Ochre and White

Lavender: Cobalt Blue, Cadmium Red Light and White

Warm White: White with a tiny amount of Yellow Ochre and Thalo Yellow Green

Use a #32 flat brush to put in the gray and lavender shadows and shadow leaves on the upper left side of the flower arrangement.

Put in the folds of the drape with gray and lavender. Add some White to these colors for variation. See the color illustration.

Use long strokes for the folds, following the lines of the drape.

Draw a line of lavender for the table edge. Then use lights and darks along the line to make it look natural. Some medium will be necessary but don't thin the paint too much. You want a rich (painty) look.

Fill in the light part of the drape and background with warm white.

Using the flat of the brush cut around the edges of the shadow leaves on the left.

Add a few strokes of Thalo Yellow Green in the edge of the arrangement on the upper right side. These strokes will brighten the real leaves and catch light.

Mix a wash of Sap Green and turpentine to make a dark green. Dab in the darkest areas around the roses. After this step you will no longer be using turpentine except to wash brushes.

PINK ROSES

Mix the following:

Lavender: Cobalt Blue, Alizarin Crimson, White

Deep Rose: Alizarin Crimson, White

Light Pink: Cadmium Red Light, White

Light Peach: Cadmium Red Light, Cadmium Yellow Light, White

Use the #32 brush to put in the lavender flowers. These flowers are not very structured. They are just a few strokes for petals. Add a stroke or two of light pink for highlights.

Use the deep rose in the shadow areas. See the color illustration. Some lavender will be added for depth and coolness. The #32 flat brush is right for this step. Move all strokes toward the stem. Use some medium as necessary. The long stem of pink flowers at the top is done with the same colors. Use a #22 flat brush for this one.

WHITE ROSES

Do the centers of the roses with little dashes of deep rose color. Allow a bit of pale green wash to show through.

Under paint the shadows in the flowers with pale lavender on the cool side and pale pink on the warm side.

Mix Thalo Yellow Green, Cadmium Red Light and White to make a light neutral color. Add some of this for background color also. Use a #22 brush for underpainting.

With a #32 flat brush form the petals. Make a creamy paint from Brilliant Yellow Light and Medium. Use little or no medium for underpainting.

The center and back petals are small dashes. On the sides the strokes are drawn toward the front and slightly down. All main petals move toward the stem, that is down from the top and up from the bottom. Don't make long strokes. Use short ones lessening the pressure on the brush in order for the background color to show through. Use medium in the top layers of paint.

VASE

Cover the vase with Brilliant Yellow Light. Crisscross in lavender and gray on the sides for shadows. Use a #32 flat brush.

Add tiny bits of yellow, green and blue to the center section. This gives the vase a slightly iridescent glow. Use medium very sparingly. Work the colors together smoothly.

Highlight with dabs of White. Make sure that you have a gray line under the vase to "sit" it down.

The rose on the table has a lavender line around the bottom for shadow also.

LEAVES

Mix three shades of green

Cool Dark Green: Sap Green and Cobalt Blue

Medium Green: Sap Green, Yellow Ochre

Light Green: Sap Green, Cadmium Yellow Light, White

There are very few really formed detailed leaves in the arrangement. Most leaves are dabs or diagonal strokes.

Leaves should be relaxed. They should not be pointing straight up or straight out.

Use the dark green in places of deepest shadow and on the left side. Add some White in this area. Use a #2 flat brush.

Leaf strokes should start at the front point. Swing the brush in a pivot toward the center.

The warmer greens are used on the right or bright side of the picture.

Add tiny bits of red to the leaves to soften the greenness. And now you are finished.

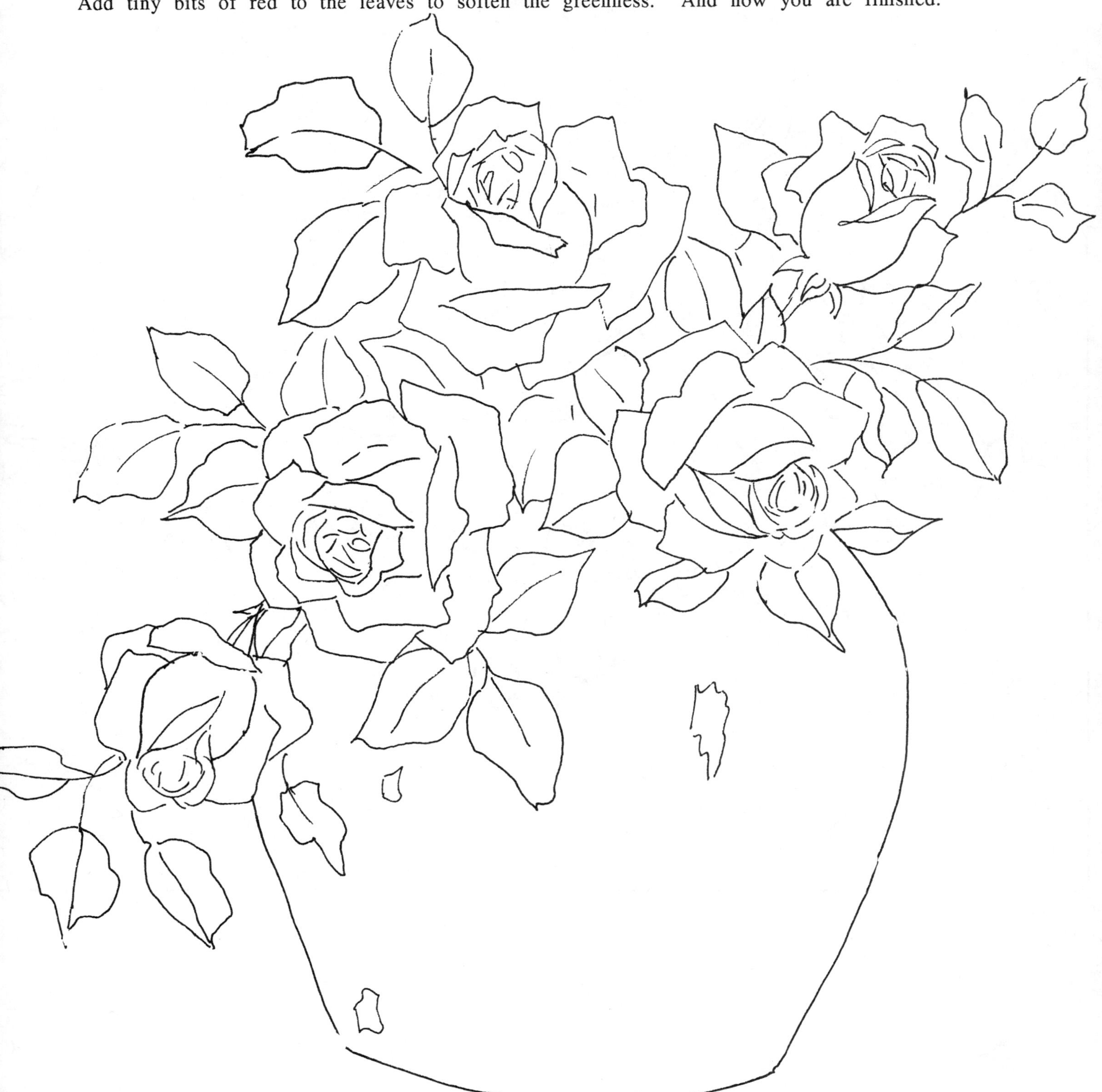

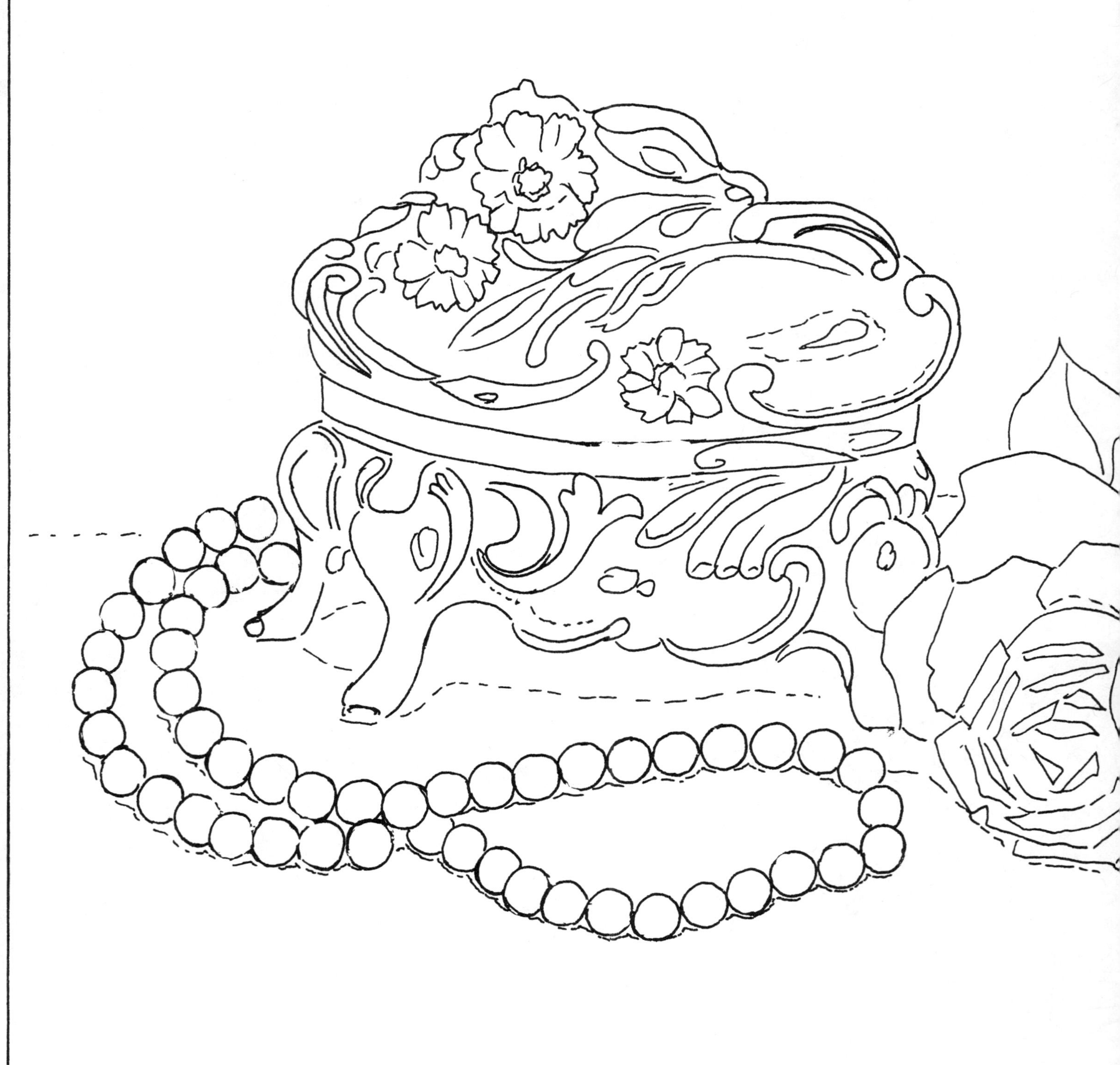

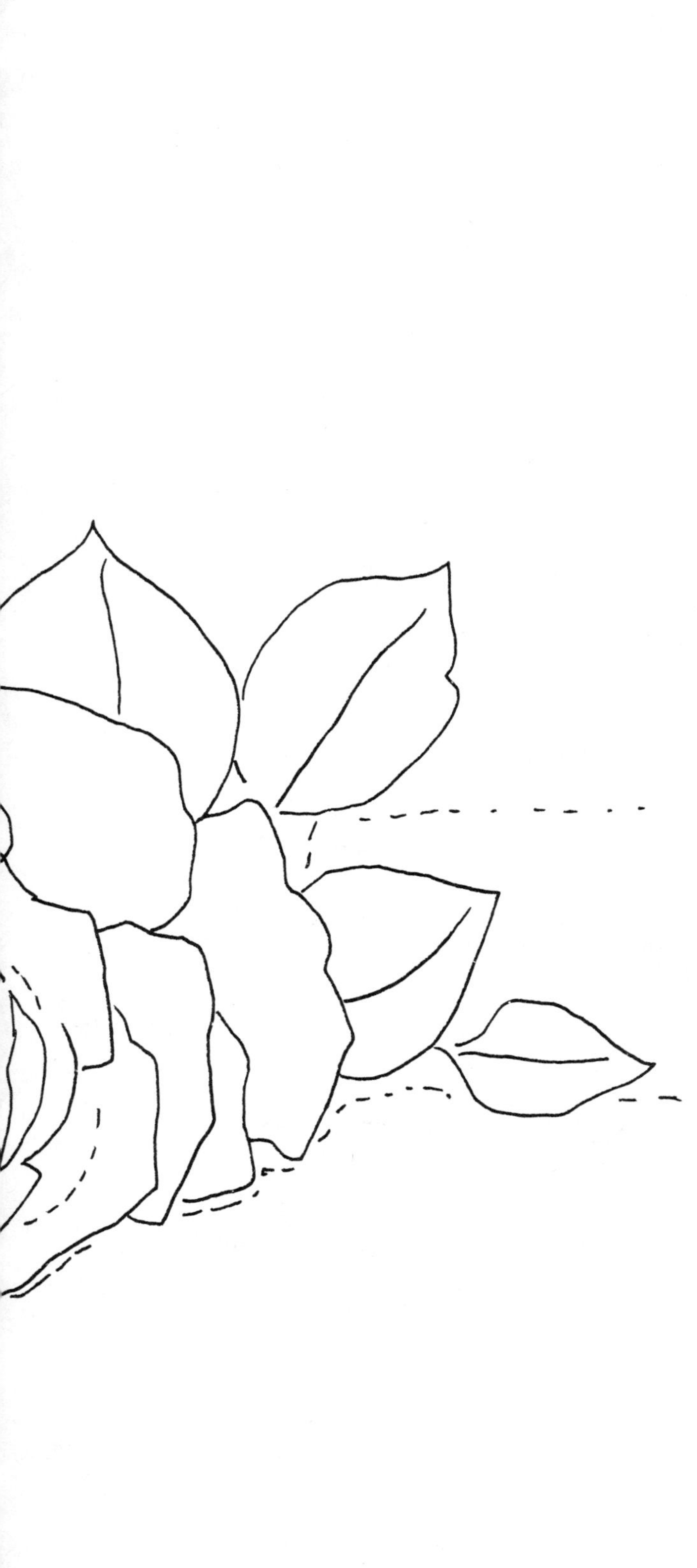

THE JEWELRY BOX

BRUSHES
Flat Sables #32,18,16, 4, 2
Spotter #1

MEDIUM: Stand Oil Light or L.O.T.
Turpentine
CANVAS: 9 x 12

PALETTE
White
Cobalt Blue
Cadmium Red Light
Yellow Ochre
Alizarin Crimson
Thalo Yellow Green

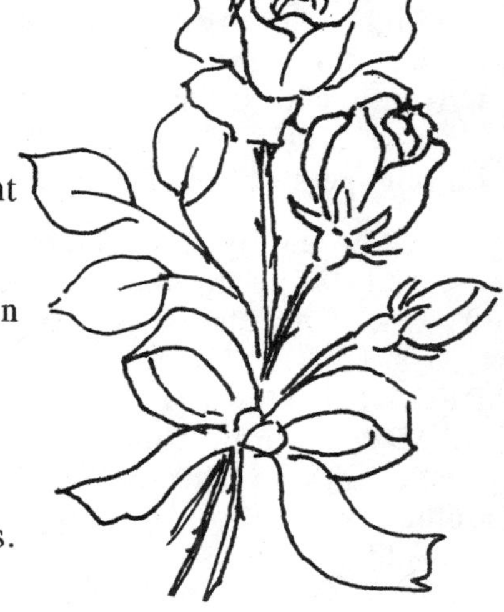

Trace pattern on canvas.

BACKGROUND

Mix a medium warm gray from Cobalt Blue, Cadmium Red Light, Yellow Ochre and White.

This basic gray can be varied by adding more or less of each color. Add White for lighter shades. This is excellent shadow material for any picture.

Use a #32 flat brush to cover the background and table with this color. Add some pink over the gray background on the right center fading it out into the gray..Use crisscross strokes.

Warm some White with a tiny bit of Yellow Ochre. Add some horizontal strokes of this to the table top in front of the rose and pearls.

SILVER BOX

Paint in the darks of the silver box with dark gray. Add White to the gray for a middle tone. Use a #16 flat brush to cover the basic box. Work some White into the highlight areas. Use crisscross strokes to blend.

Mix the following colors for the reflected lights.

Medium Blue: Cobalt Blue and White

Light Yellow: Yellow Ochre and White

Rose: Alizarin Crimson and White

Add these little bits of color to give the basic color some sparkle. See the color illustration for this. Use a #2 and 4 brush for the details.

For the final highlights add warm white with a palette knife. Use a knife with a rounded end not more than 1/4 inch wide at the point. A rough dab will do.

Add very dark gray under the box for shadow.

THE JEWELRY BOX

LEAVES

Mix Cobalt Blue and Thalo Yellow Green to make a dark blue green.

Cover the leaves with this color using a #18 flat brush. Mix White with this color for lights.

Add tiny bits of Cadmium Red Light for accents. Use a #2 flat sable for this.

ROSE

Prime the area with turpentine tinted to a light green with Thalo Yellow Green. Allow this to dry or almost dry. Turpentine evaporates rapidly.

Mix the following:

Deep Rose: Alizarine Crimson and White

Light Pink: Cadmium Red Light and White

Do the center first. Use a #16 flat brush to put in deep rose with tiny accents of Alizarine Crimson and Cadmium Red Light. A tiny bit of green will enhance these colors.

Use a #18 flat brush to cover the basic areas of the rose. Put in the deep rose shading to pink on the petals. Add bits of light gray from the background in shadows. Use little or no medium.

Allow a tiny bit of the Thalo Yellow Green wash to show at the base of the bud.

Add White to the wet pink to produce highlights. Blend lightly with a #16 flat brush.

Use a #4 flat brush to add Alizarine Crimson accents to the edges of the petals.

PEARLS

Mix a warm white from White and a tiny amount of Yellow Ochre.

Put in the shadows under the pearls first. Use the darkest gray and a #2 brush. Use a slightly lighter shade for the gray shade on the pearls.

Add a light side using warm white. Use a #4 flat brush for the basic color.

Add dabs of pink, pale yellow and pale blue on each pearl. Put on a White highlight.

Frame out each pearl with light gray around the top.

The pearls in front of the box should be the lightest and brightest. Let them become grayer and cooler as they recede into the shadows. The more you work them the better and more real they will become. This is a picture for detail lovers.

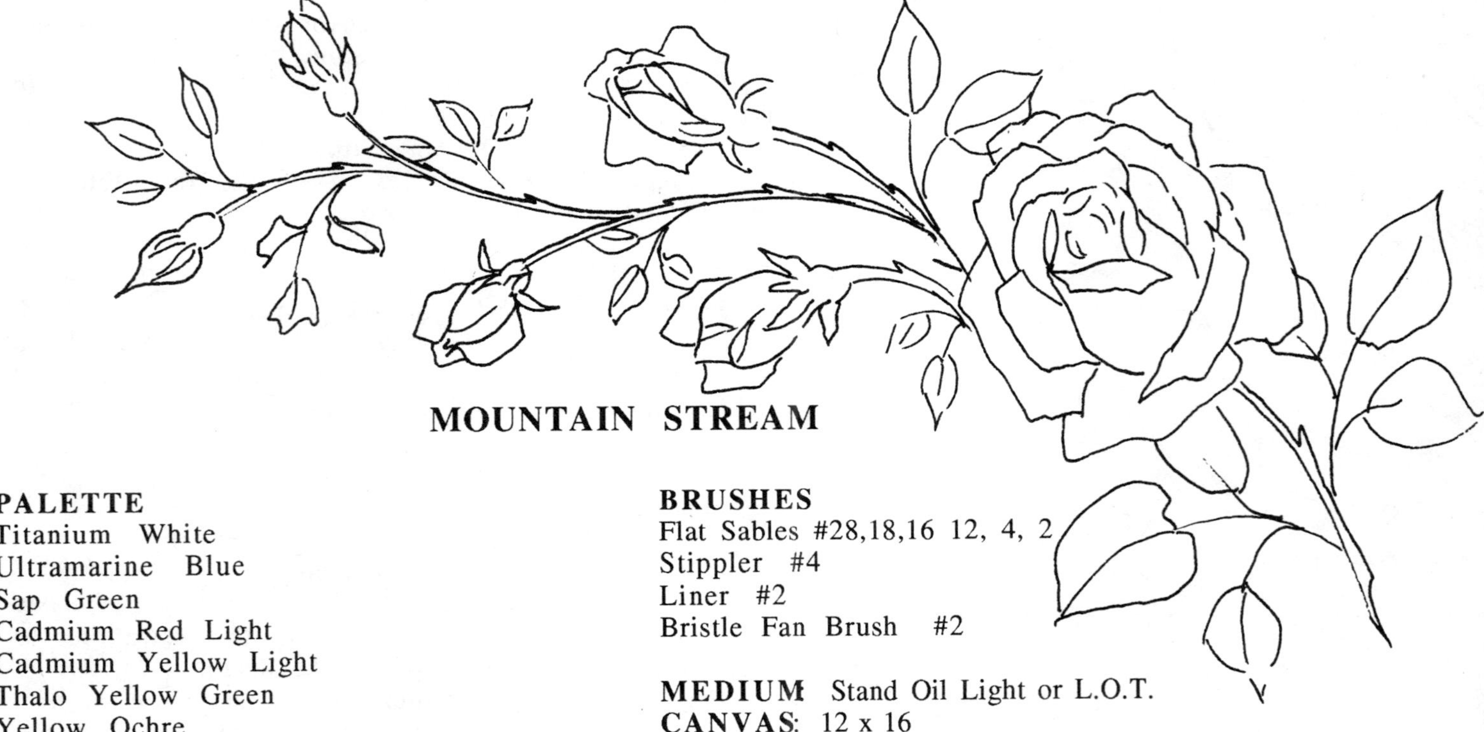

MOUNTAIN STREAM

PALETTE

Titanium White
Ultramarine Blue
Sap Green
Cadmium Red Light
Cadmium Yellow Light
Thalo Yellow Green
Yellow Ochre

BRUSHES

Flat Sables #28,18,16 12, 4, 2
Stippler #4
Liner #2
Bristle Fan Brush #2

MEDIUM: Stand Oil Light or L.O.T.
CANVAS: 12 x 16

Trace the pattern on the canvas.

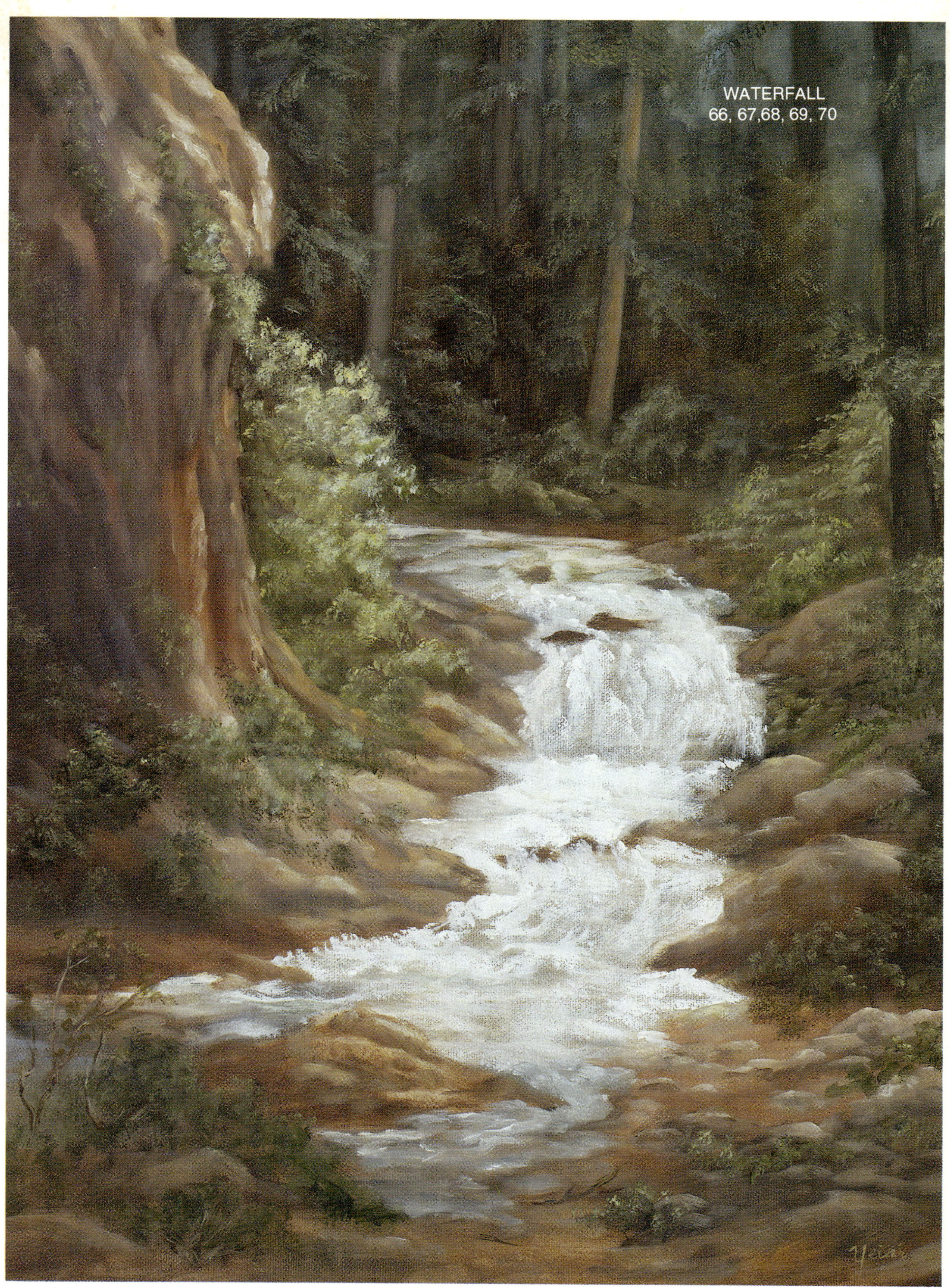

WATERFALL
66, 67,68, 69, 70

THE PORCH CAT
14, 15, 16, 17

STILL LIFE WITH PITCHER
22, 23, 24, 25

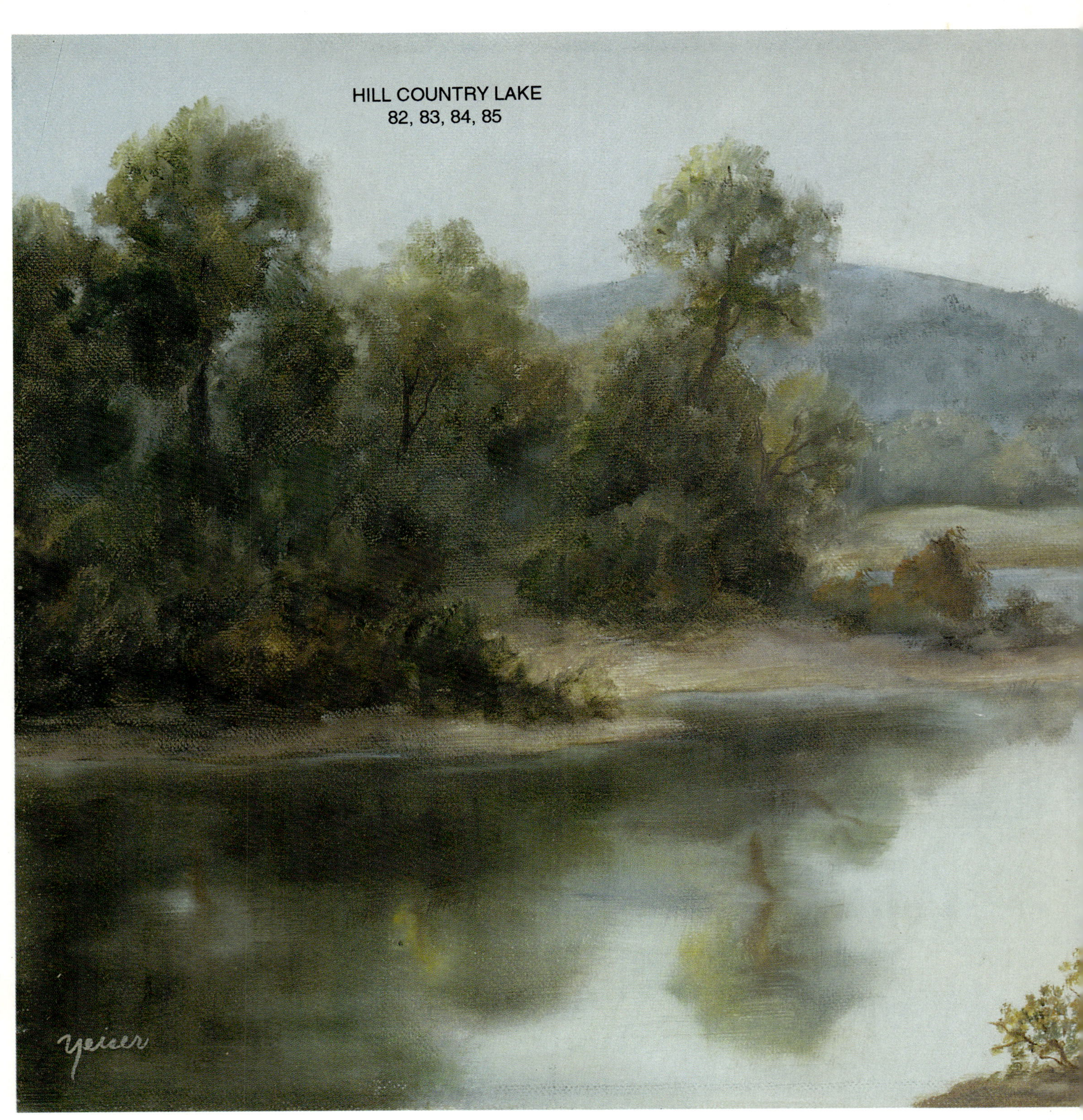

HILL COUNTRY LAKE
82, 83, 84, 85

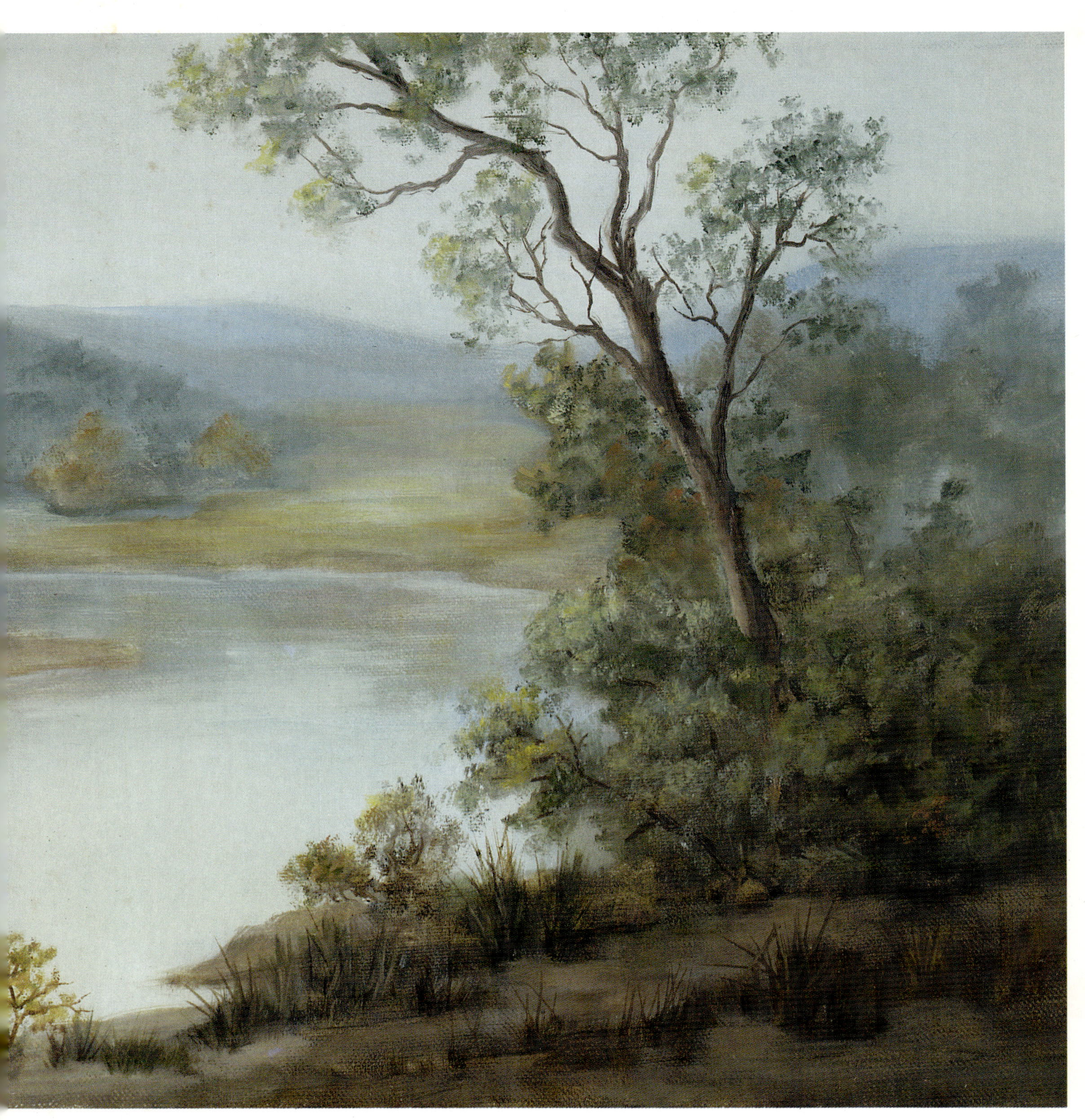

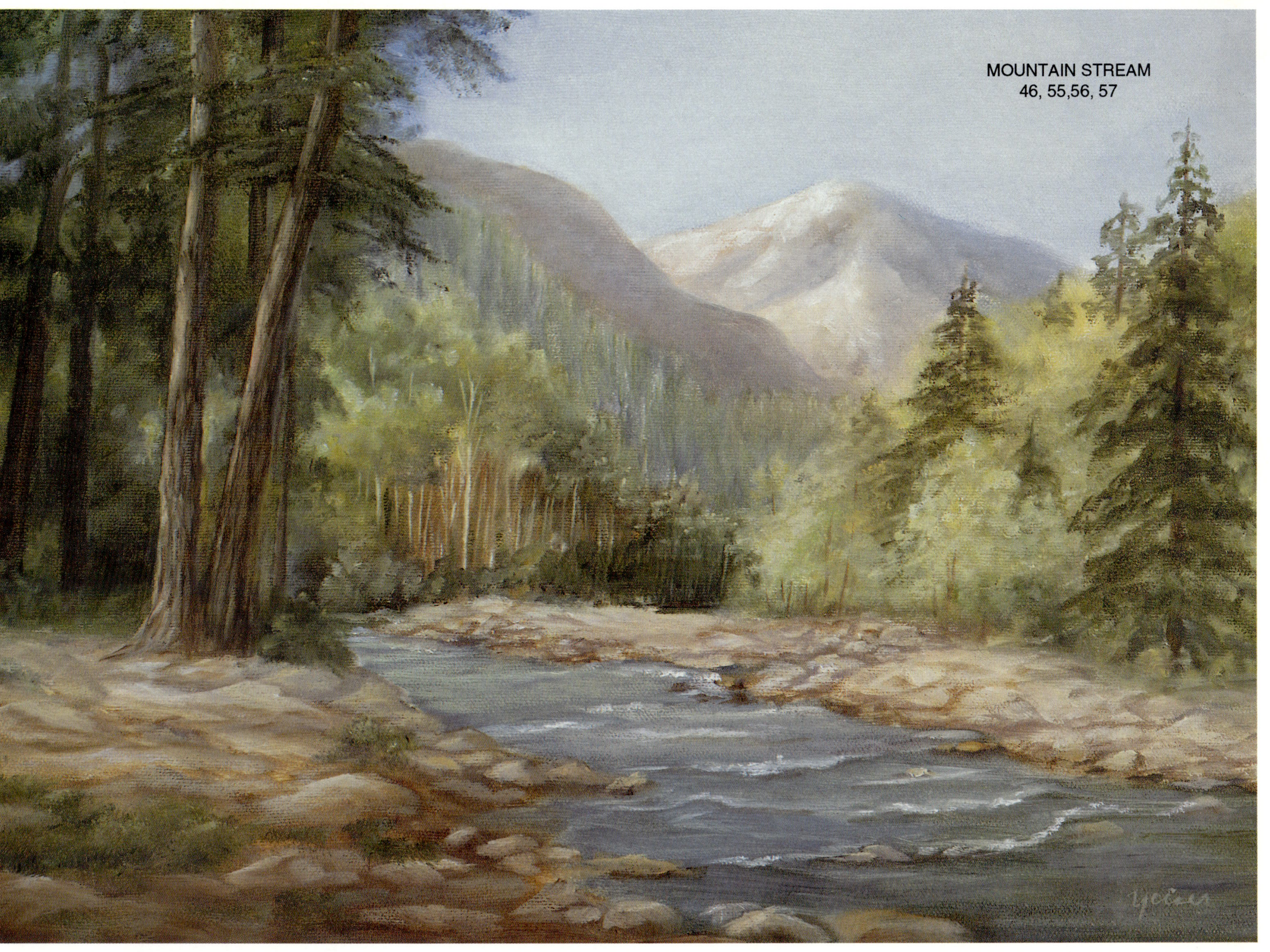

MOUNTAIN STREAM
46, 55,56, 57

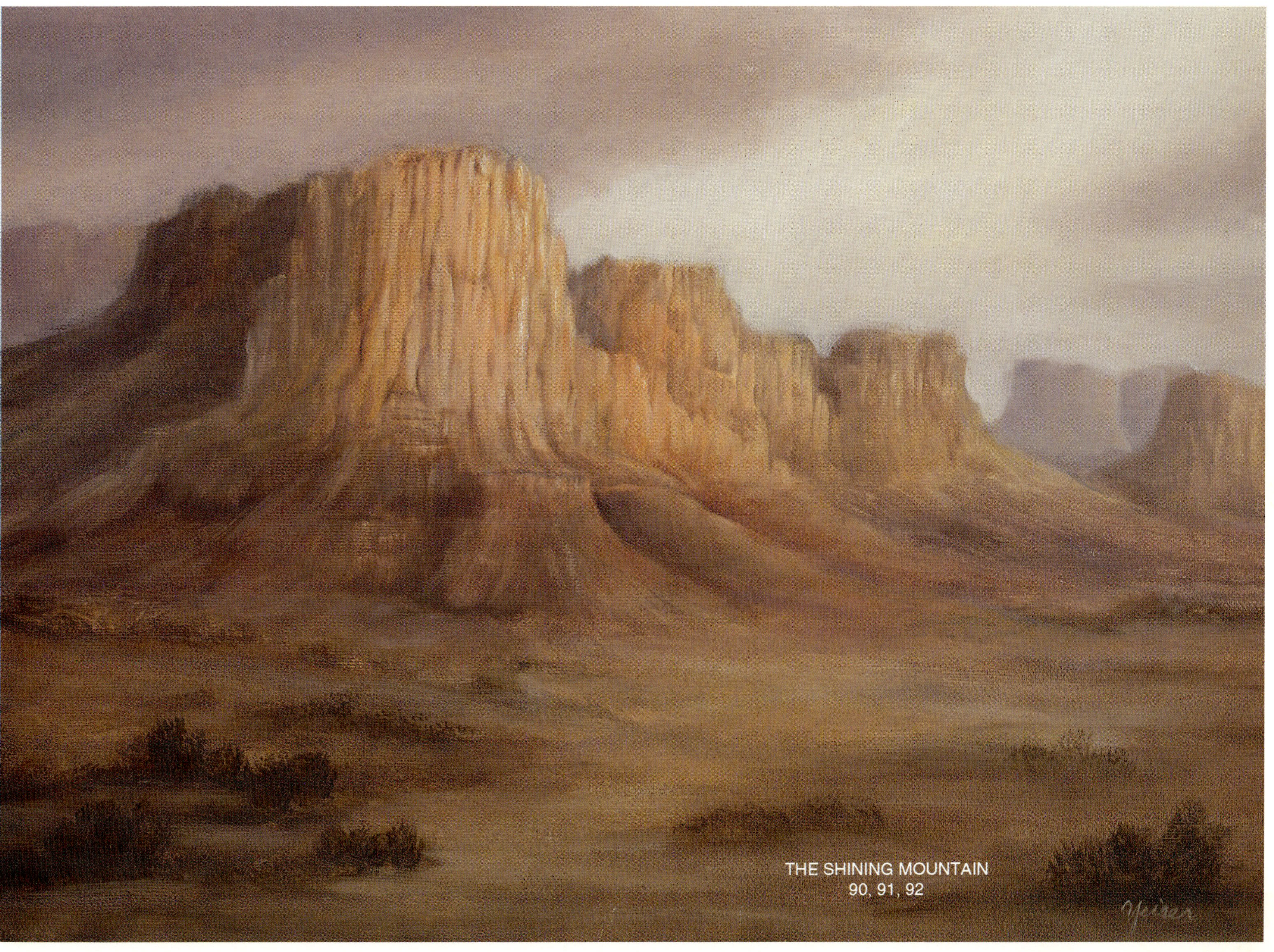

THE SHINING MOUNTAIN
90, 91, 92

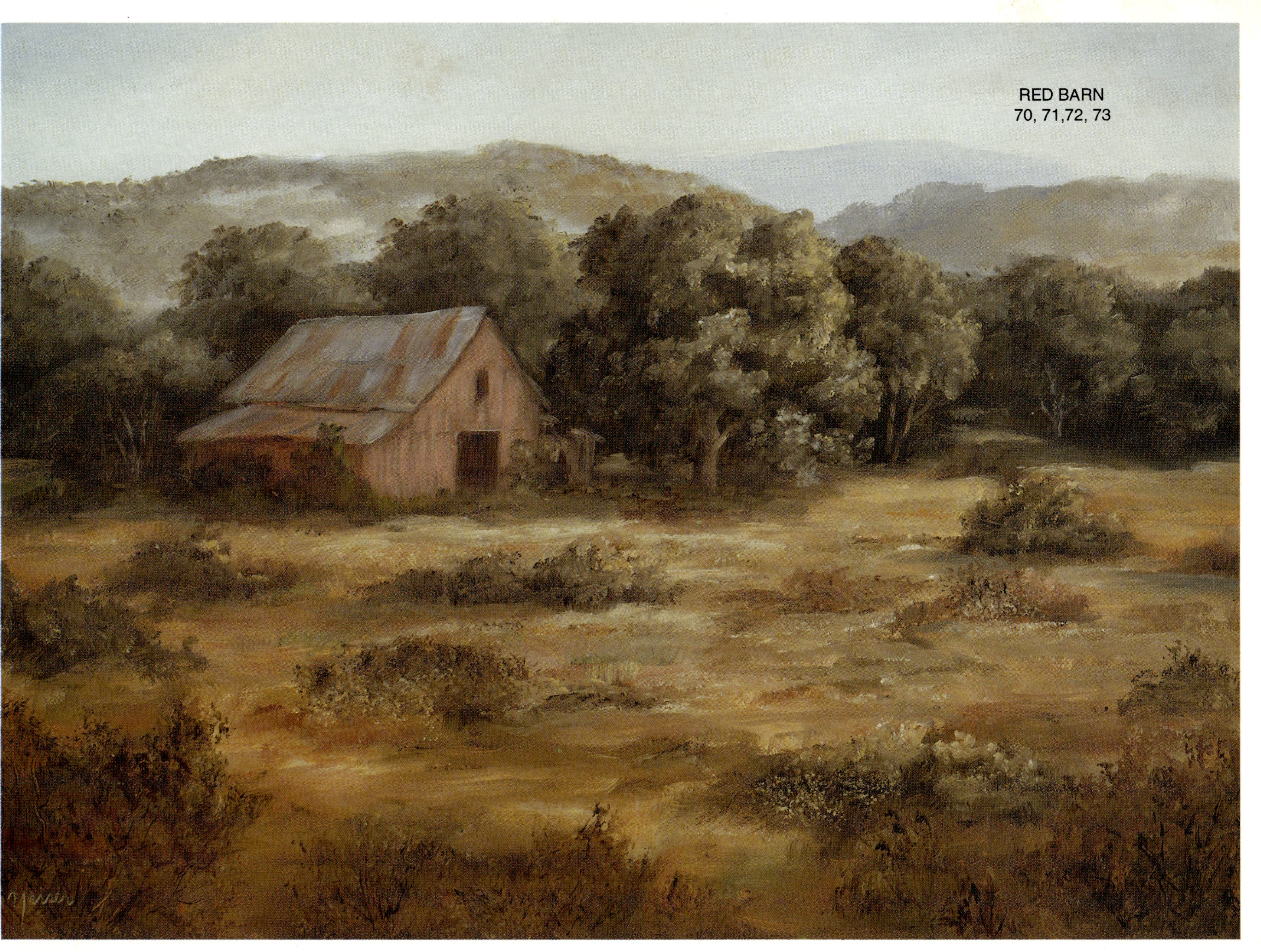

RED BARN
70, 71,72, 73

SKY

Mix Ultramarine Blue and White to make a light blue. Paint the sky light blue using a #18 brush. Crisscross in some white blending it into the blue. The corner should be darker than the center. Darker corner keeps the eye in the picture. Use Stand Oil or L.O.T. sparingly.

MOUNTAINS

Mix the following colors:

Light Peach: Cadmium Red Light, Yellow Ochre, White

Medium Blue: Ultramarine Blue, White, and a touch of Cadmium Red Light

Cover the distant mountains with medium blue on the shadow side. Use the same blue for the shadows on the light side. Cover the light side with peach. Use a #16 brush for covering. Add some thick rough strokes of White for snow on this side.

The second mountain (on the left) shows only the shadow side. Cover this with dark peach. Allow this color to rest for awhile and go over it with medium blue leaving a slight peach glow underneath.

BACKGROUND TREES

Mix a medium blue green from Ultramarine Blue, Sap Green and White. Fill in the trees against the mountain using a #12 flat brush. Vertical strokes are needed here. This color will be repeated in the water.

Mix a dark blue using Ultramarine Blue, White and a touch of Sap Green. Use this color for the background behind the tall trees on the left side. With a #18 flat brush dab in theis area. You may want to use th corner of the fan brush for the lacy edges of the tree tops. Use some medium as needed.

Mix the following colors:

Dark Green: Sap Green, Ultramarine Blue

Medium Green: Add White to dark green

Light Yellow Green: Thalo Yellow Green, White

Warm Yellow: Cadmium Yellow Light, Yellow Ochre, White

Dab in a few splotches of medium and light green behind the tall trees across the center of the canvas.

Mix Yellow Ochre with a touch of Burnt Umber and White for the small area just left of the center. This is background for the stand of birches. Add the white trunks with the edge of a #2 flat or a #1 liner.

Put a bit of light yellow green on the tops of the trees against the mountain. With a #4 flat use a soft touch to get an indistinct distant look.

Put in the dark green firs on the right. Draw in th truck with Burnt Umber toned with Yellow Ochre. Dab in the foliage with a #2 fan brush. Add the other small dark trees at this time. Use the #2 stippler to put in the highlight of warm light yellow on the band of trees across the center background.

TALL TREES

With a #4 brush put in the dark trunks Burnt Umber softened with a bit of Sap Green is fine for the darks. Use peach color (from the mountains) for the lights on the trunks.

Pat on the dark green foliage with the flat end of a #18 flat brush or use the #2 fan brush. Pat on a bit of medium green for highlight.

WATER

Begin the water with blue green from the background trees gradually progressing to dark blue green. Use horizontal strokes with a #18 flat sable brush.

Over these colors add in the background lights or yellow green and some mountain colors. Finally add White for foam.

In the lower right corner put in some earth tones. Give the horizontals a rippling effect to indicate running water.

Dab in some dark green bushes among the rocks and your are finished.

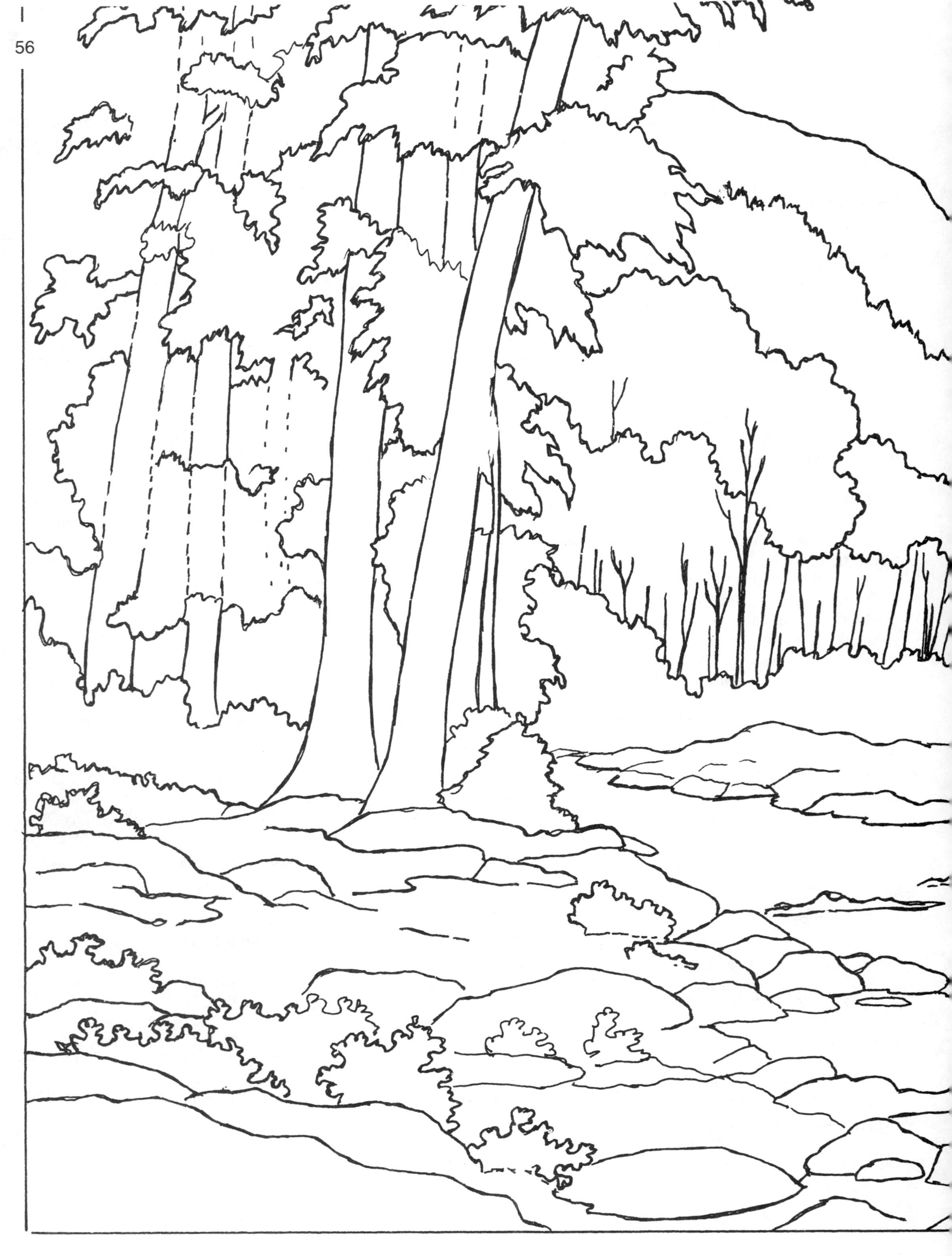

MOUNTAIN STREAM

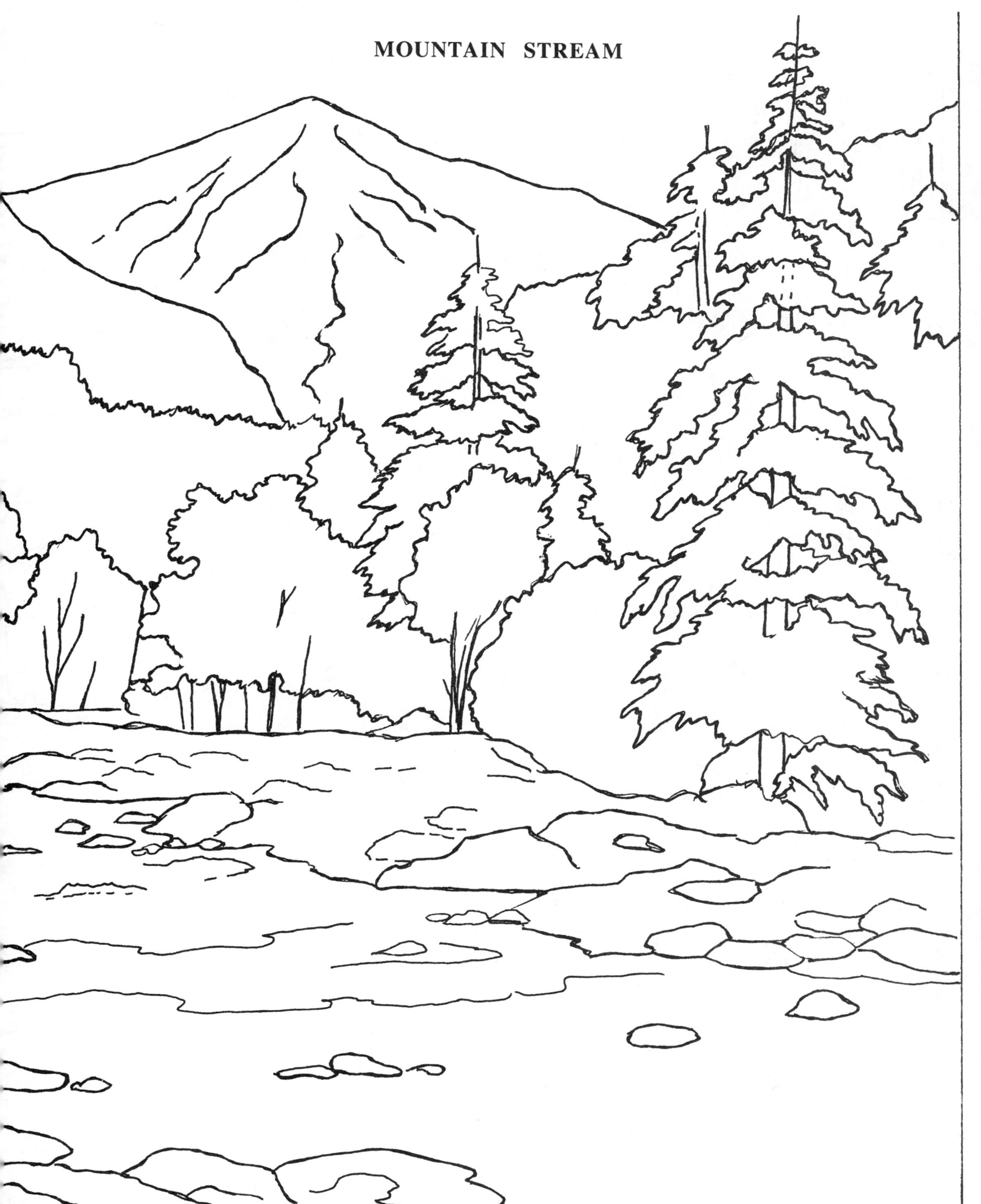

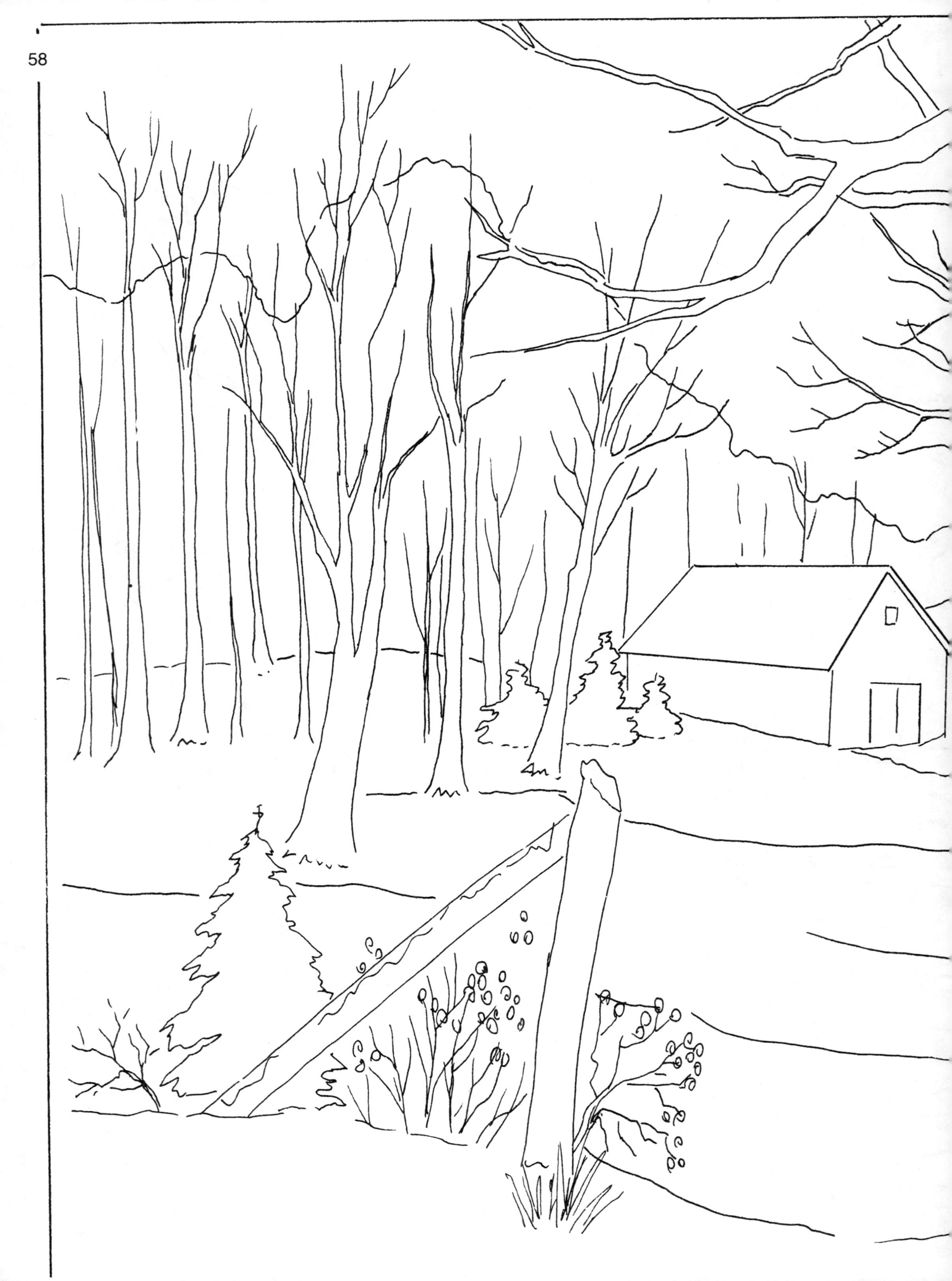

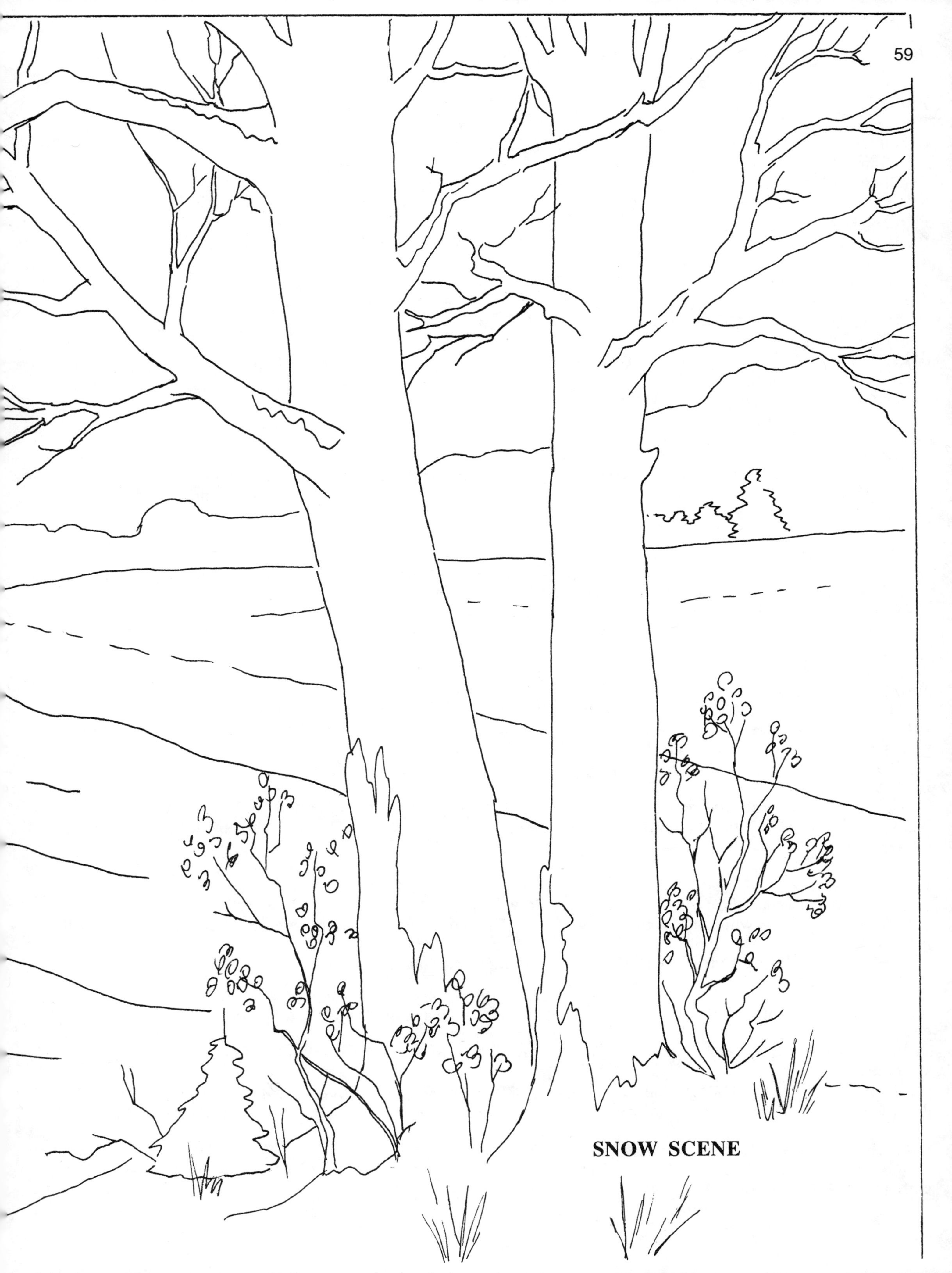

SNOW SCENE

SNOW SCENE

PALETTE
White
Cobalt Blue
Cadmium Red Light
Cadmium Yellow Light
Raw Umber
Paynes Gray
Raw Sienna
Viridian Green
Alizarin Crimson

BRUSHES
Flat Sable #32, 18, 16, 4, 2
Liner #1

MEDIUM: Stand Oil Light of L.).T
Turpentine

CANVAS: 12 x 16

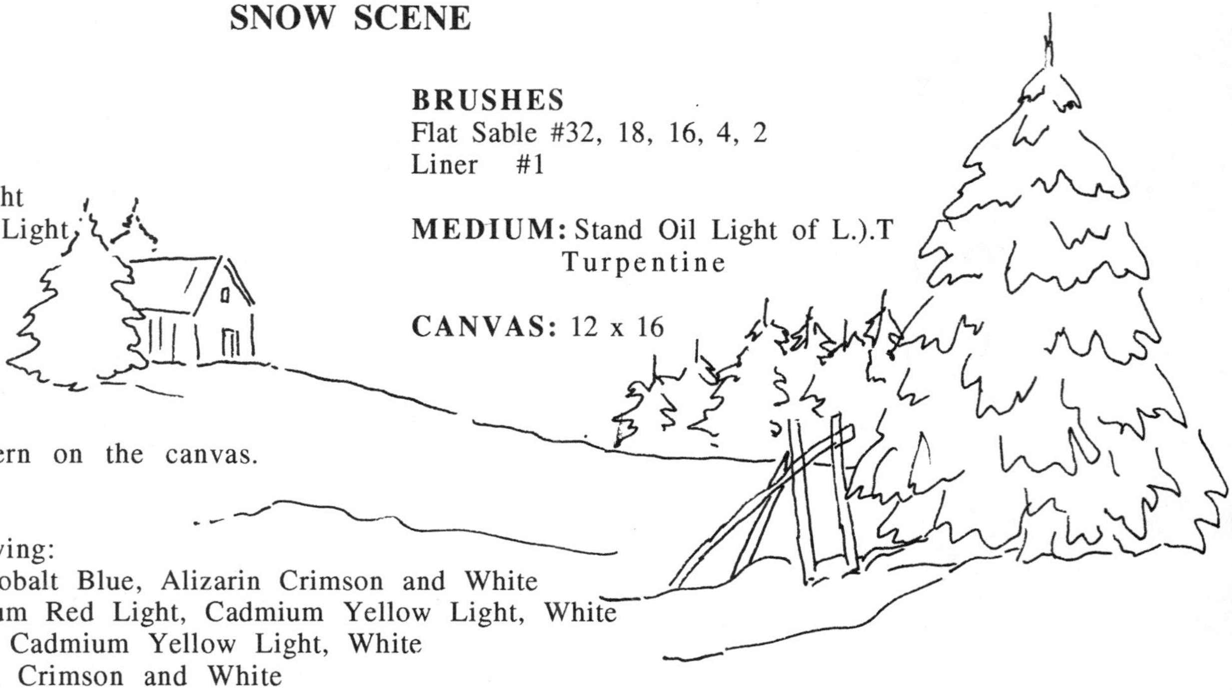

Trace the pattern on the canvas.

SKY

Mix the following:
Light Blue: Cobalt Blue, Alizarin Crimson and White
Peach: Cadmium Red Light, Cadmium Yellow Light, White
Light Yellow: Cadmium Yellow Light, White
Pink: Alizarin Crimson and White

With a #32 flat brush paint the top 2/3s of the sky with light blue using crisscross strokes.

Gradually fade into the pink and peach color. Add a dash of yellow for the sunrise. Add some peach behind the trees.

DISTANT TREES

Use the sky color for the distant trees in the center. A #16 brush will do for this small area.

Mix a medium gray from Paynes Gray, Raw Umber and White.

With a #18 flat brush cover the tree areas. Use vertical strokes. Fade the tops into the sky. With a deeper shade of gray add small trunks and limbs. Use a #2 flat brush and a #1 liner for the small things.

SNOW

Mix more light blue from Cobalt Blue and White. Cover the snow areas using horizontal strokes with a #32 flat brush. Use White for the lighter areas. Add peach highlights in the appropriate places. See the color illustration.

BUILDING

Cover the roof with sky color. Add some peach light at the top. Use a #16 flat brush.

Paint the front of the building with medium gray from the trees. Add the shadow side with a darker gray.

LARGE TREES

Mix a warm black from Paynes Gray and Raw Umber.

Cover the trunks with this color using a #18 flat brush for the large areas. Vertical strokes will help to create a "barky look".

Add vertical streaks of gray and peach to lighten the black.

Put in the main limbs with a #16 flat brush. Use a #2 and #4 flat and a #1 liner for the smaller limbs. When using a liner thin the paint to an almost liquid consistency so that the liner will carry it.

Allow the limbs to dry if you like before you add the snow. Use White with a bit of peach for sparkle.

When doing the middle ground trees on the left side, add more light streaks to the black to push them further back. Lighter values recede. Use a #4 flat brush and a #1 liner for the limbs.

SMALL EVERGREENS

Add some Cobalt Blue to the Viridian Green to make a blue green. Dab in the small green trees with the # 4 flat brush. Add dabs of White and peach for snow.

BUSHES

Use a #2 flat brush for the large parts. Add the small limbs with a #1 liner.

Mix Raw Sienna and Cadmium Red Light to make a rust color for the leaves on the bushes. Add some yellow or peach for variety. Dab this on with a #4 flat brush.

FENCE POST

Use the black and gray to cover the post. Add streaks of peach and light blue. A #16 flat brush will be right for this step. Top with White and peach snow.

Add grass with a #1 liner. Mix Raw Sienna and White to make this color.

After everything dries add the bit of barb wire using the #1 liner.

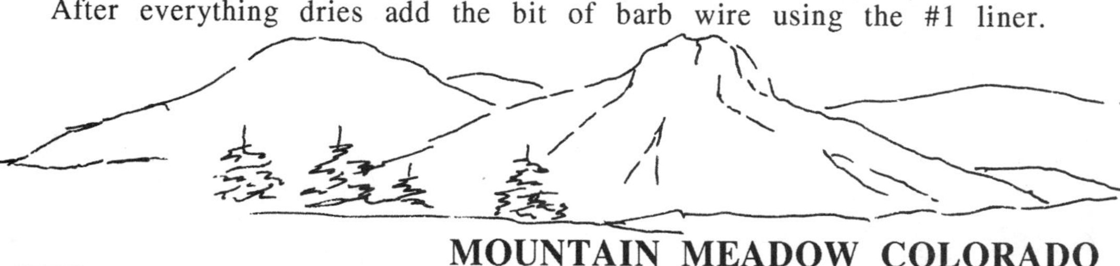

MOUNTAIN MEADOW COLORADO

SKY

Mix the following

Light Blue: Cobalt Blue, White

Light Blue: Cerulean Blue, White

Paint the top of the sky with Light Cobalt Blue. Use a @32 flat brush. Add a strip of light Cerulean Blue for the middle sky. Paint the bottom 1/3 with Brilliant Yellow Light and Permalba White. This makes a warm white. Other brands are too yellow for this area.

Use rough crisscross strokes to blend the areas together. This will overlap the colors to give you a cloud effect. Use some Stand Oil or L.O.T. as needed

MOUNTAINS

Mix the following

Medium Warm Blue: Cobalt Blue, Cadmium Red Light, White

Light Peach: Cadmium Red Light, Yellow Ochre, White

Light Blue Green: Cobalt Blue, Sap Green, White

Cover the cool side of the mountains with medium blue Use a #18 flat brush Use the light blue in the warm sunny side of the mountain.

Add some White and light peach to the distant mountains using a #12 flat brush.

For the center mountain add bits of White on the ridge tips.

Use the palette knife to put in the rough lights for snow. White will be needed for the shady side and very pale peach on the sunny side.

Add the light blue green at the base of the mountain for trees.

HOUSE

Mix a dark gray with Raw Umber and Cobalt Blue. Add White to make a lighter gray. Use streaks of these colors on the house. Apply with a #4 flat brush. Do the window with dark gray.

ROOF

Mix Burnt Sienna, Cadmium Red Light and White to make a red brown. Pat in this colors with a #12 flat brush. Streak with bits of gray, a few lines of Raw Umber for seams. Follow the roof line with the strokes. The house is not perfectly straight since is has settled with age.

FIELD

Mix the following

Warm Brow: Raw Sienna, Burnt Sienna

Start at the back of the field. Use a #2 fan brush to pat in light yellow alternating with dark yellow. As you move toward the front of the field add darker, richer earth tones. Add some greens from the trees in the foreground.

Continue to pat in different colors in rough horizontal lines. Be careful not to make the horizontals too even. They should be vague and irregular. Use medium as necessary.

MOUNTAIN MEADOW COLORADO

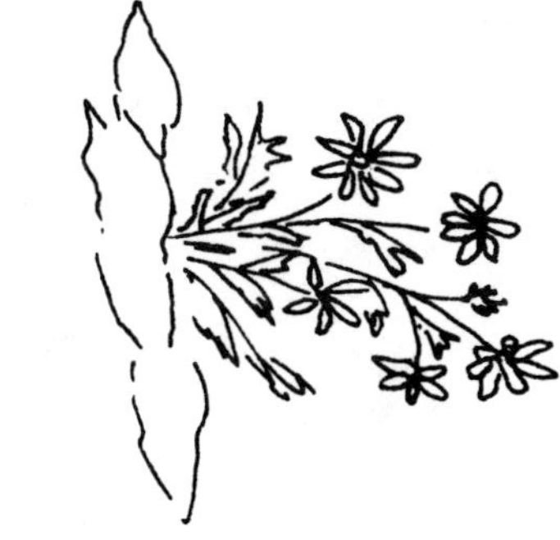

PALETTE
White (Permalba)
Brilliant Yellow Light
Cobalt Blue
Cerulean Blue
Cadmium Red Light
Yellow Ochre
Cadmium Yellow Medium
Sap Green
Raw Umber
Raw Sienna
Burnt Sienna

BRUSHES
Flat Sable #32, 28, 12, 4
Stippler #3
Fan #2

MEDIUM Stand Oil Light or L.O.T.
Turpentine Odorless

CANVAS: 14 x 18

Trace the pattern on the canvas. Prime the bottom half of the canvas with turpentine tinted to a light brown with Raw Umber.

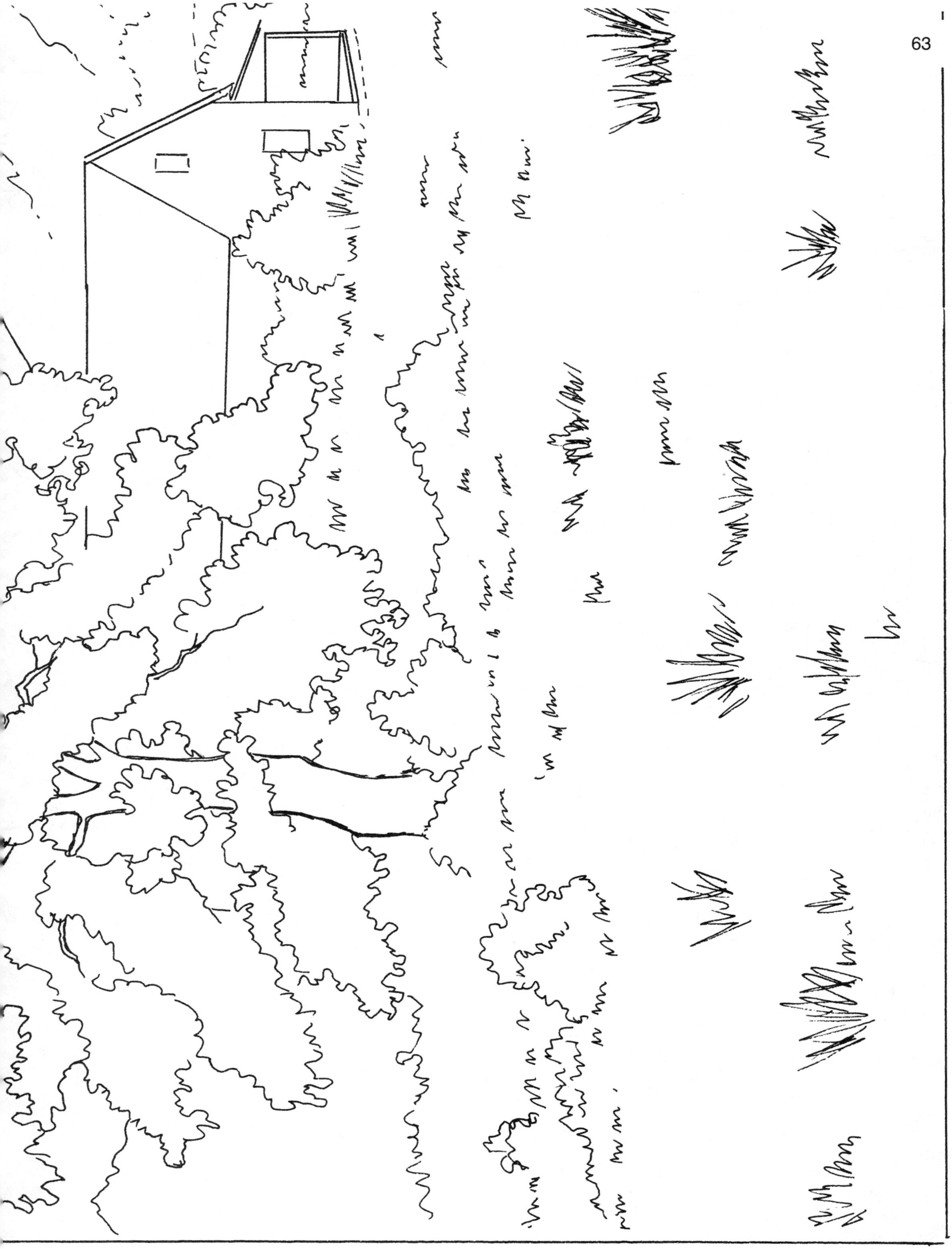

MOUNTAIN MEADOW COLORADO

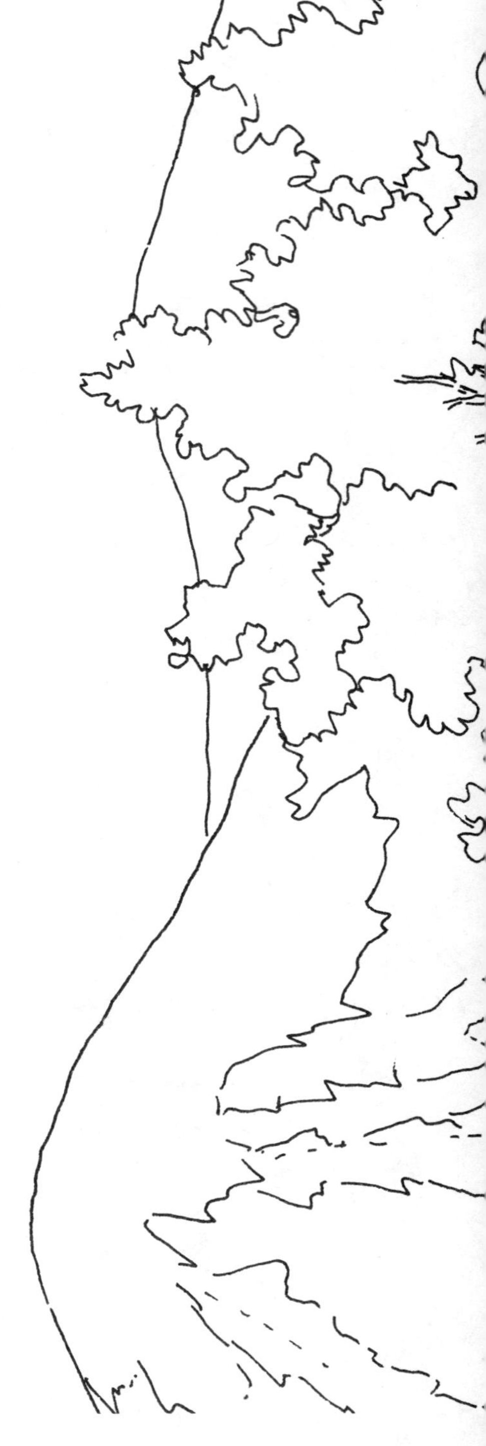

TREES

Mix the following

Cool Dark Green: Sap Green, Cobalt Blue, White

Medium Green: Sap Green, Cobalt Blue, Yellow Ochre

Light Green: Yellow Ochre, White, Sap Green

Use a #12 or #16 flat to dab in the dark green for the background trees. Dab on the medium green for highlights.

Add small trunks and limbs with brown (Raw Umber and White). Use a #2 flat brush or a #2 liner for the small limbs.

Put in the trunk and limbs of the main tree before putting in the foliage. Use Raw Umber for the darks and highlights with the roof colors while the Raw Umber is wet.

Use a #3 stippler to do the foliage. Put in the dark green first. Add the medium green and the light green last of all.

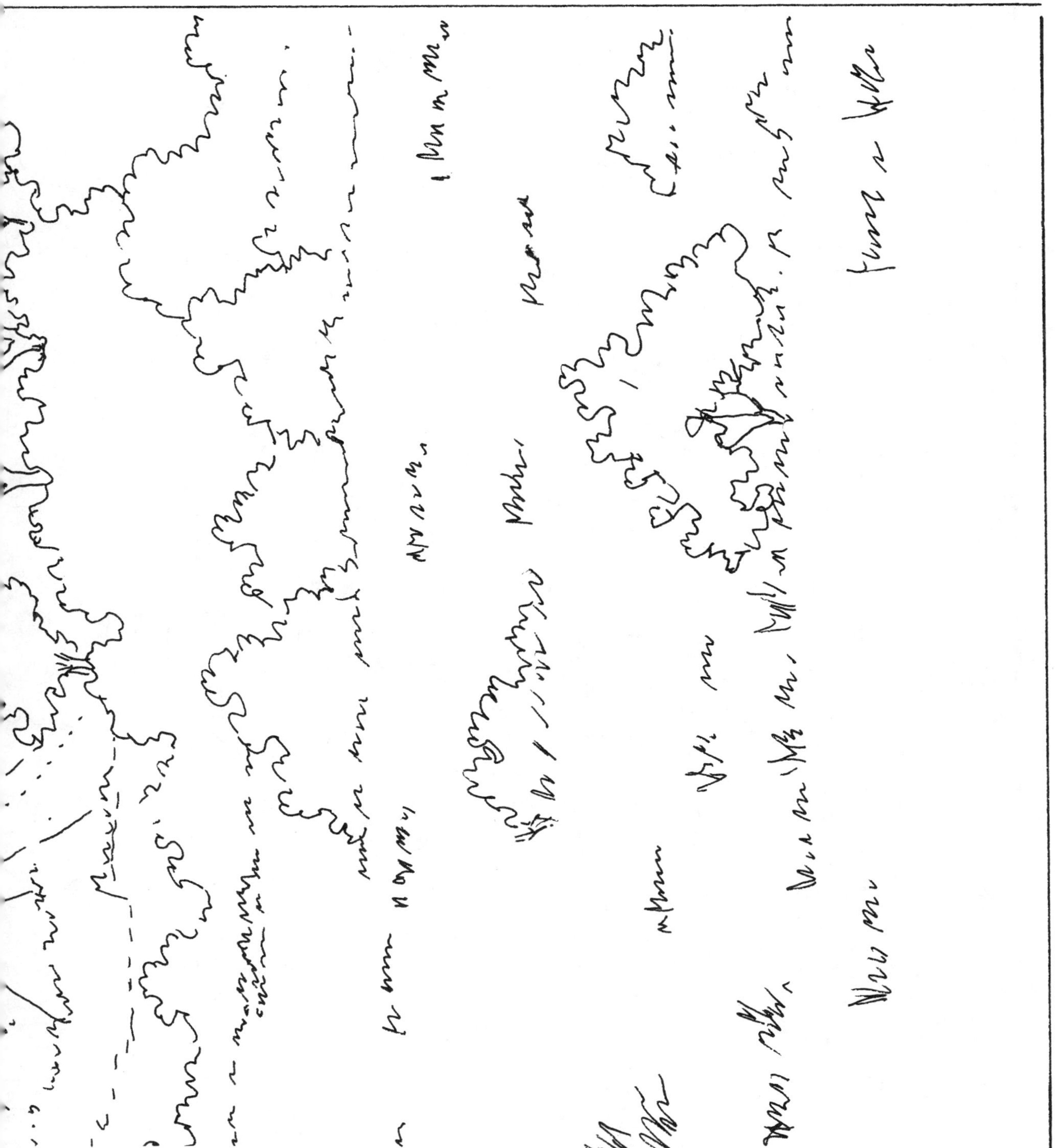

BUSHES AND GRASSES

Add dark green weeds and bushes under the main tre. Use the fan brush to pat yellow grasses over the edge of the dark greens. Dab in some small green bushes with a #4 flat.

Add some long clumps of grass with the edge of a #4 flat brush.

You are finished, enjoy.

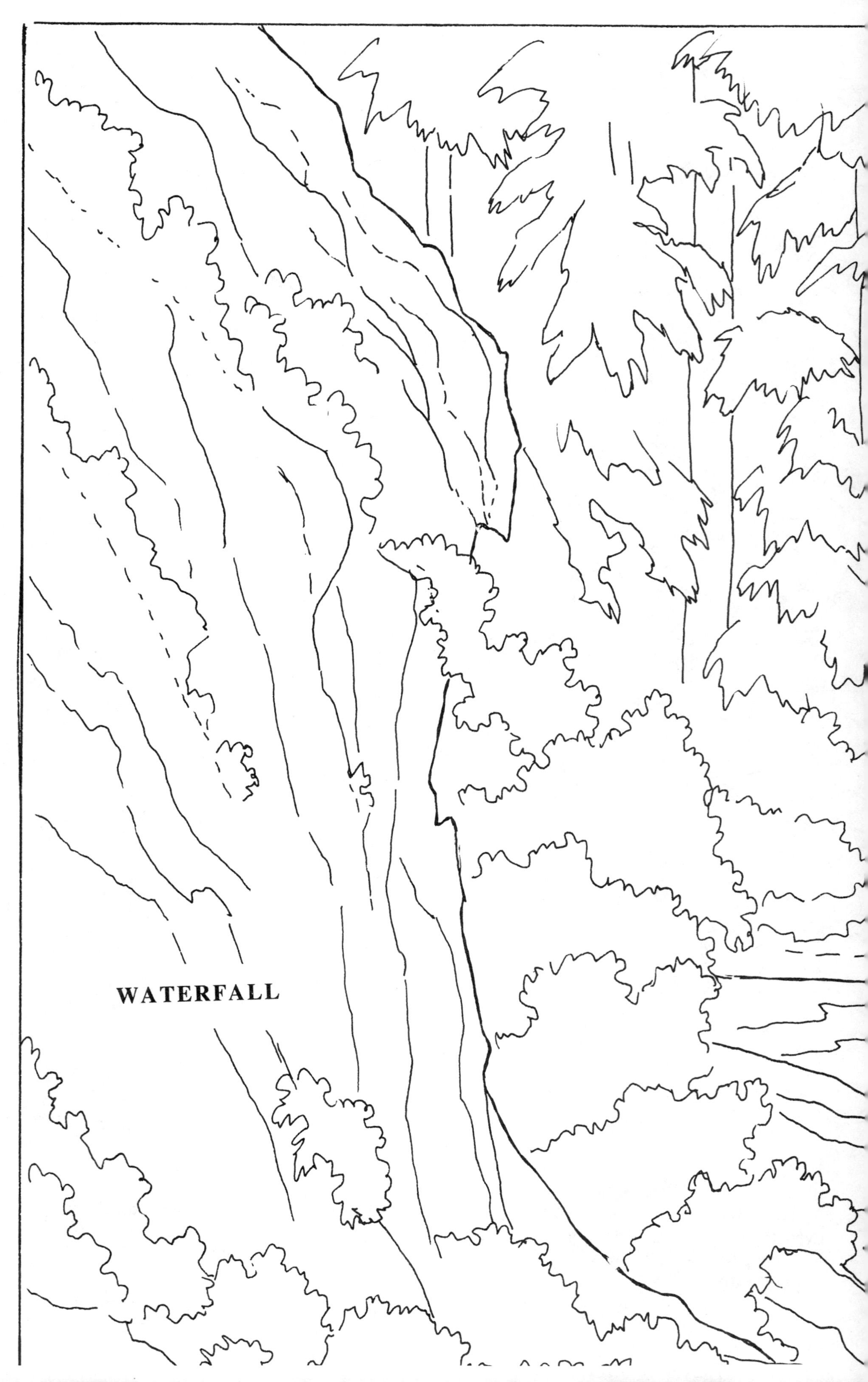
WATERFALL

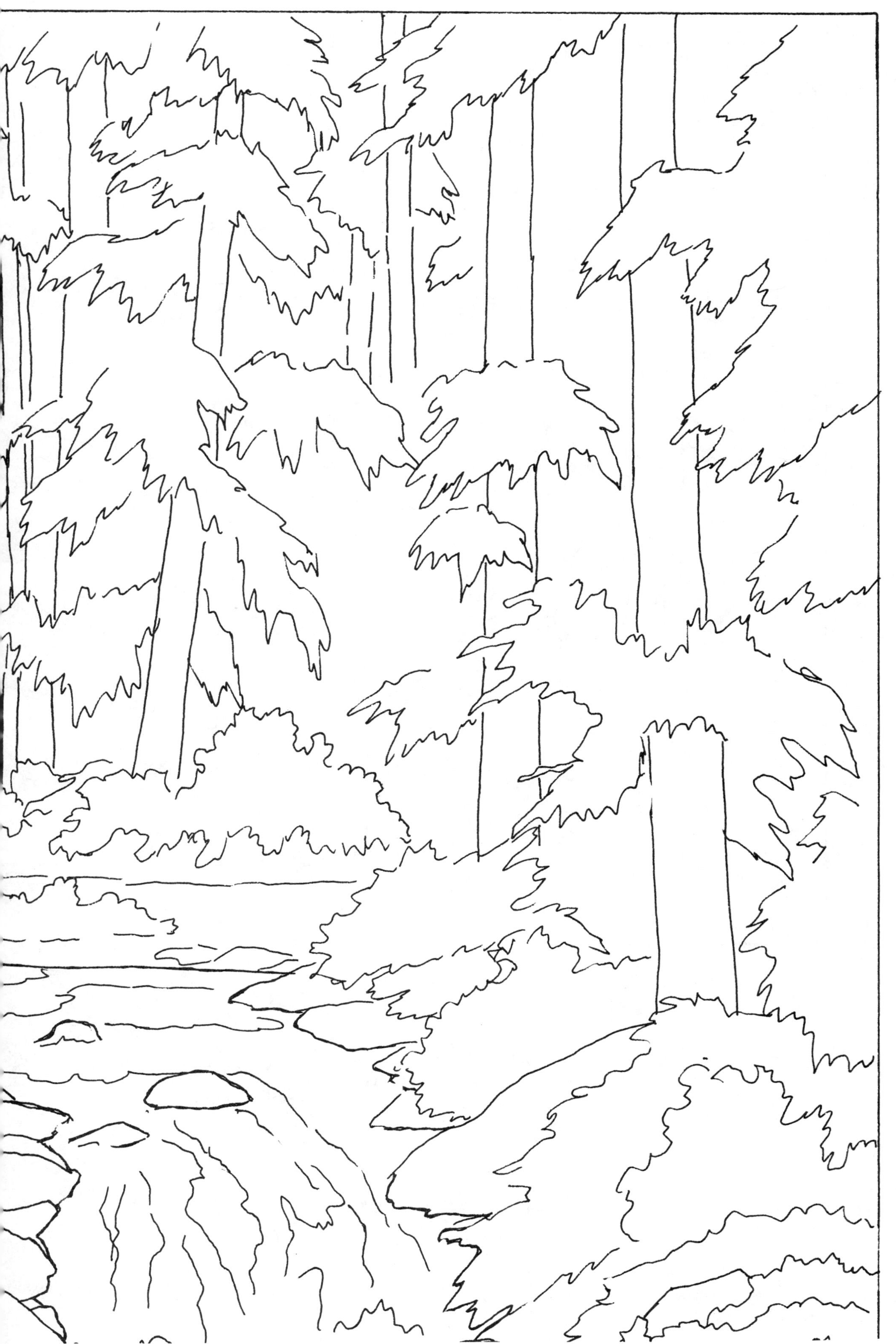

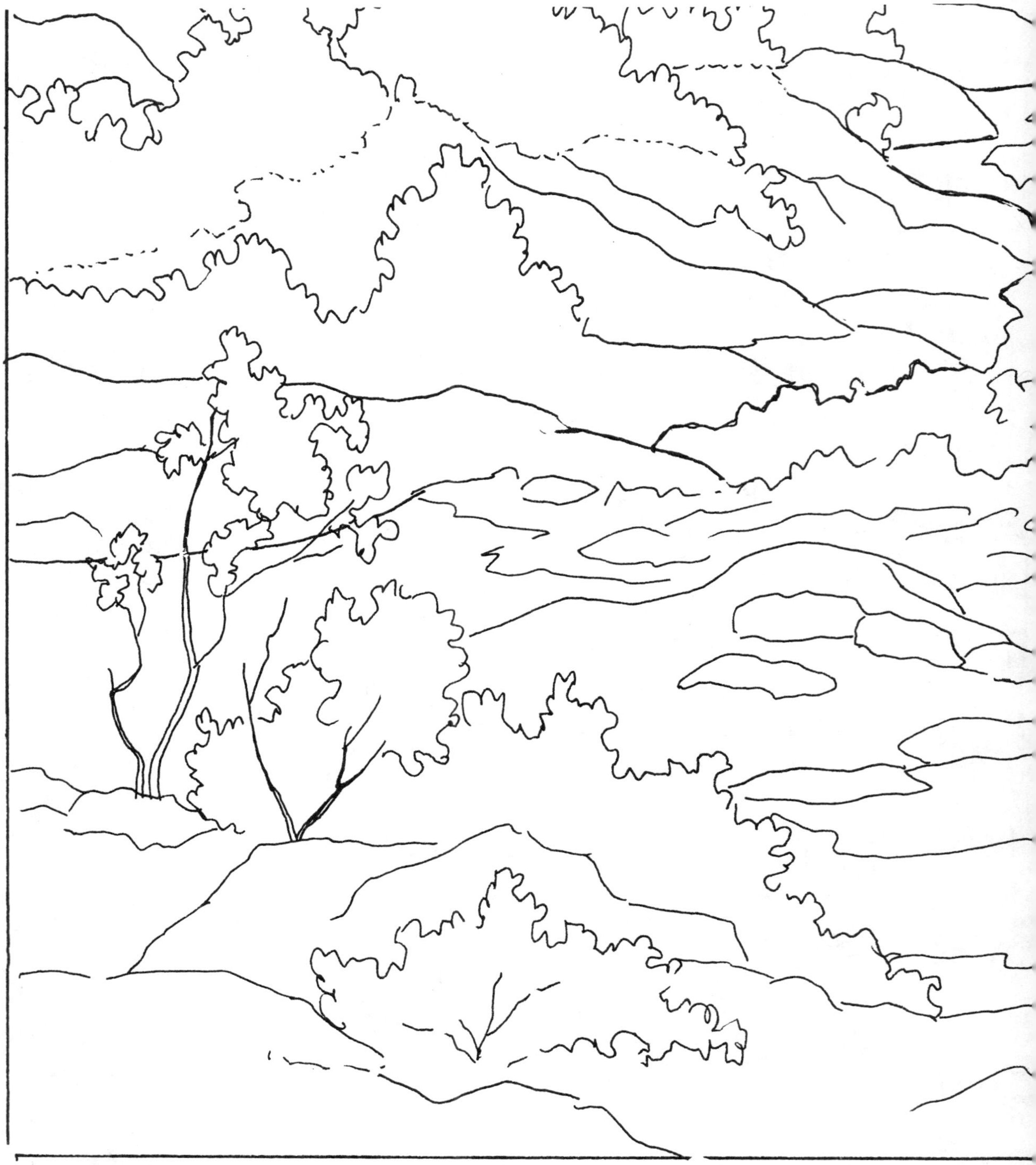

WATERFALL

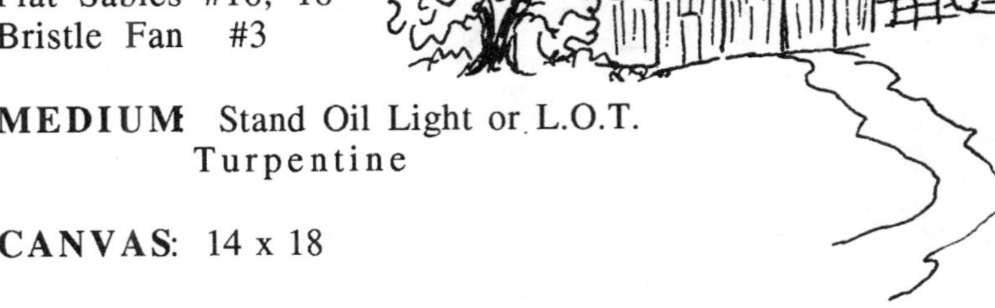

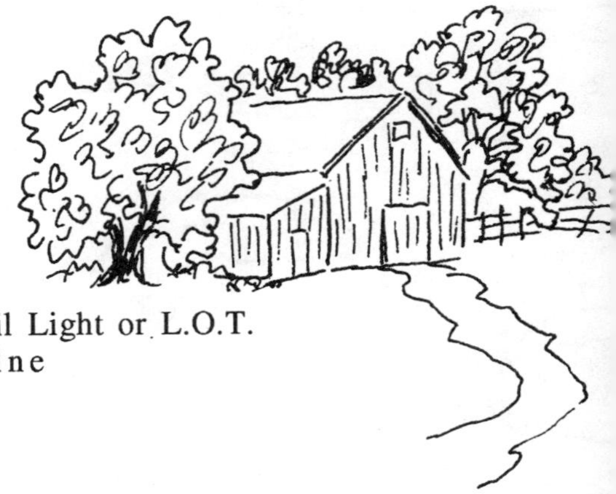

PALETTE
White
Cadmium Yellow Light
Mars Yellow
Raw Sienna
Burnt Sienna
Raw Umber
Burnt Umber
Ultramarine Blue
Sap Green

BRUSHES
Flat Sables #16, 18
Bristle Fan #3

MEDIUM Stand Oil Light or L.O.T.
Turpentine

CANVAS: 14 x 18

Prime the canvas with turpentine tinted to a light brown with Raw Umber. Allow it to dry. Trace on the pattern.

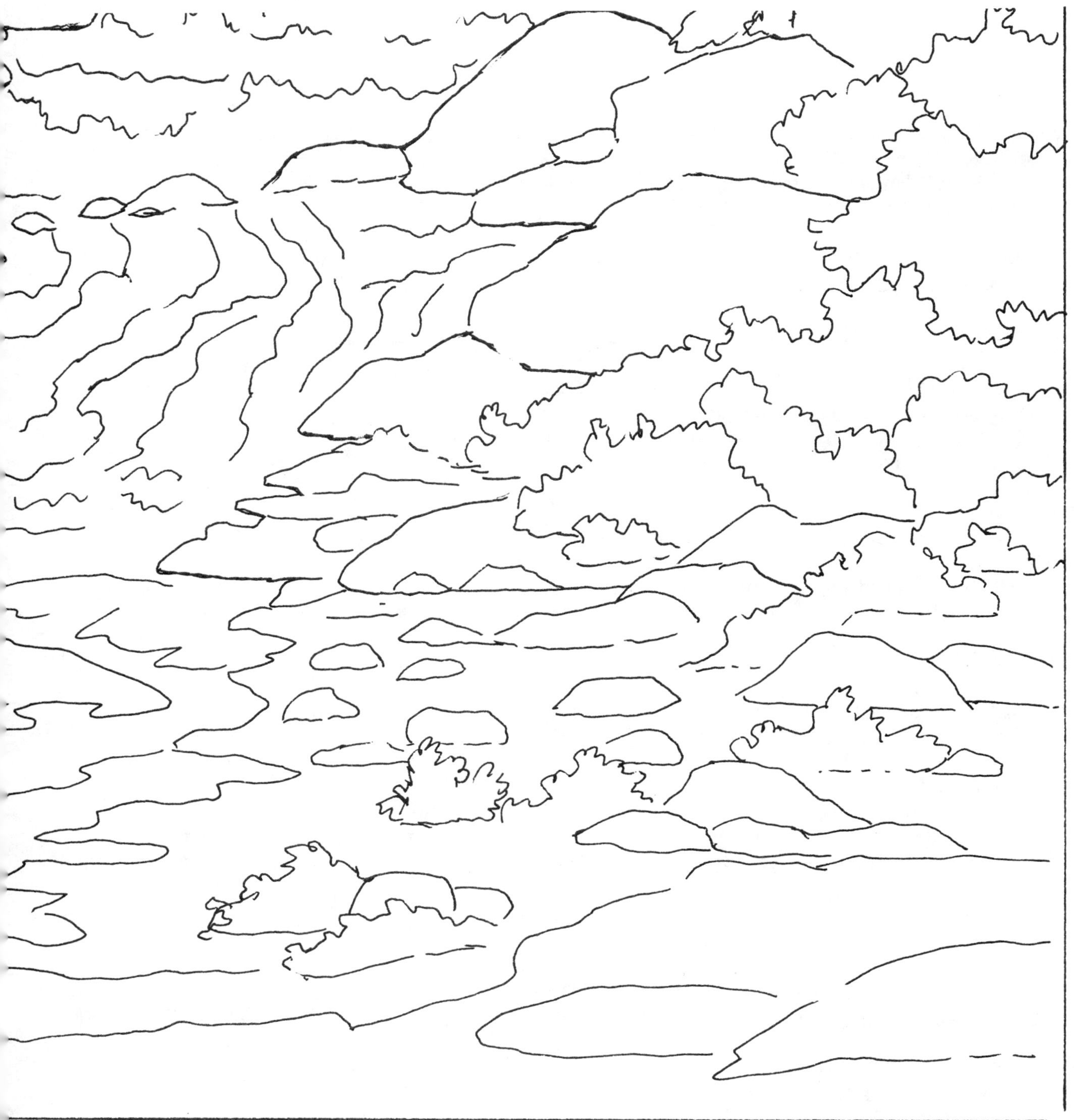

BACKGROUND FOREST

Mix the following colors:

Dark Green: Sap Green, Ultramarine Blue, White

Medium Green: Add White to the dark green

Brownish Green: Sap Green, Raw Umber

Warm Green: Sap Green, Raw Umber, Cadmium Yellow Light

Use the medium green to do the atmosphere between the tree trunks. Use a #18 brush. This can be done with vertical strokes.

Do the tree trunks with Raw Umber. Add dark green to the Raw Umber for the darkest trunks and medium green to the the Raw Umber for lighter trunks.

The two tree trunks in the center section will have earth colors added later. Use a #16 brush with vertical strokes for the trunks.

Dab in the foliage with a #18 brush using the various shades of green. A #3 bristle fan brush may be used for the drooping limbs, earth cliff and rocks. Paint the waterfall area with the medium green. Use horizontal strokes. You will add the White foamy water later.

WATERFALL

CLIFF

Mix the following: Cool Browns
Dark Purplish Brown: Burnt Sienna, Ultramarine Blue and White
Medium Cool: Raw Umber, White
Gray Brown: Burnt Umber, Ultramarine Blue and White
Blackish Brown: Burnt Umber, Ultramarine Blue

Mix the following Warm Browns:
Red Brown: Burnt Sienna, White
Brown: Burnt Umber, White
Tan: Raw Sienna, Mars Yellow, White

Put in the darks, middle tones and lights in this order. The darks will be the purplish brown. If you need a few really dark accents use the Blackish Brown.

As each area emerges from the shadows use middle tones to lights.

Use a #18 flat brush and generally follow the vertical lines of the cliff.

ROCKS AND EARTH

Add the horizontal rocks around the water using the same earth tones but there are fewer really dark shadows here.

Again you will be using darks, middle tones and lights. Use a #16 brush and mostly horizontal strokes with some dabbing on the highlights. The rocks in the water are dark because they are wet.

BUSHES

Mix three shades of green:
Dark: Sap Green, Raw Umber and White
Medium: Sap Green, Mars Yellow
Light: Cadmium Yellow Light, Sap Green and White
Dab in the foliage and the light green bushes with a #16 flat brush.

Use these three shades starting with the dark and progressing to middle tone and then light.

Use the cooler green background greens for the bushes in the shadows and on the vines on the cliff.

WATER

Add the white foam over the background color. Use a #16 flat brush.

At the very back of the stream, use horizontal strokes. After the first fall use vertical strokes. Make them a little wiggly. Pat in little dabs of spray and foam. Be careful not to cover all the dark base coat.

Add some blue grays (Ultramarine Blue, Burnt Umber and White) at the bottom left so that the water won't run out of the picture. Now you are finished. This picture came from a photograph taken by my son Joseph Daniel and I would like to give my thanks for the contribution.

RED BARN

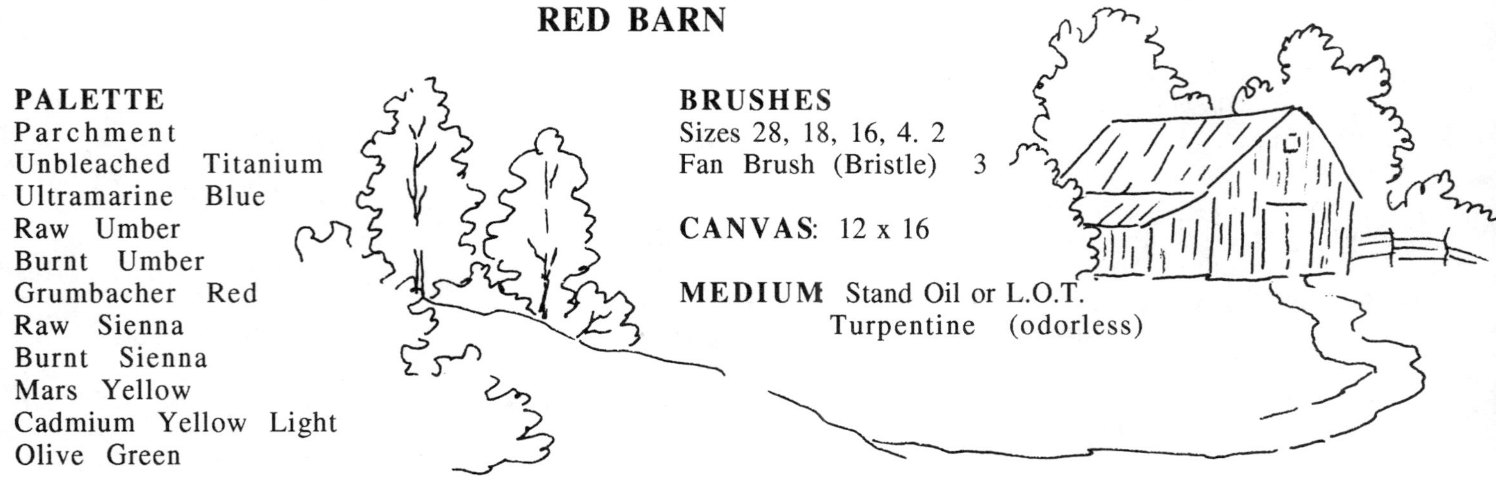

PALETTE

Parchment
Unbleached Titanium
Ultramarine Blue
Raw Umber
Burnt Umber
Grumbacher Red
Raw Sienna
Burnt Sienna
Mars Yellow
Cadmium Yellow Light
Olive Green

BRUSHES

Sizes 28, 18, 16, 4. 2
Fan Brush (Bristle) 3

CANVAS: 12 x 16

MEDIUM Stand Oil or L.O.T.
Turpentine (odorless)

Prime the canvas with turpentine tinted to a very light brown with Burnt Umber. Allow this to dry.

SKY

Mix a very light blue from Parchment and Ultramarine Blue. With a #28 flat brush cover the tip of the sky using horizontal strokes. For the lower part of the sky use Parchment. Dab a bit where the two colors meet for a slight cloud effect.

For the blue hill use Ultramarine Blue with Unbleached Titanium to make a very pale blue gray. A #18 flat brush and horizontal strokes will do for this. Use medium as necessary.

HILL

Mix the following colors:
Medium Blue Green: Olive Green, Ultramarine Blue and Parchment
Blue Gray: Parchment and Ultramarine Blue
Warm Tan: Raw Sienna and Unbleached Titanium

Cover the hill with Parchment using a #28 flat brush and horizontal strokes.

While this is wet dab in bits of blue green and blue gray on the shadow side (left). A #16 flat brush will be good for this step. Add dabs of warm tan on the light side. These colors will blend a little with the wet Parchment to create a soft look.

Let some of the colors overlap on the cool and light sides. Leave some bare spots.

TREES

Mix the following:
Dark Green: Olive Green, Ultramarine Blue, Parchment
Medium Green: Olive Green, Raw Umber, Parchment
Warm Green: Olive Green, Raw Sienna
Light Warm Green: Olive Green, Mars Yellow
Light Yellow: Parchment, Cadmium Yellow Light

Cover the tree area with dark green. Use a #18 flat brush and crisscross strokes for the basic shape. Dab in the soft edges with a #16 flat brush.

Dab in the medium cool green while the dark green is still wet. The left side is the cool side. Dab it in the warm green on the light or warm side.

Use the light yellow for highlights. Add this while everything is wet. You may need to add a few super lights in the middle after it dries.

The secret to layering wet paint is to put down the first layers in thin coats. Spread thin, not thinned with medium. Use medium very sparingly on the bottom layers. Add the small tree trunks with Raw Umber highlighted with Unbleached Titanium.

BARN

Cover the roof with blue gray (from the distant hill). Use a #16 flat brush Let the strokes follow the roof line. Add the details with a #4 brush.

The rust on the tin is made from Burnt Sienna and lightened with Unbleached Titanium.

The faded red on the walls is Burnt Sienna, Grumbacher Red and Unbleached Titanium. Use vertical strokes. Mix Burnt Umber and Unbleached Titanium to make a dark brown for the door and details. Use a #4 flat brush for the small stuff.

FIELD

Mix the following:
Warm Tan: Mars Yellow, Raw Sienna an Unbleached Titanium
Warm Yellow: Cadmium Yellow Light, Mars Yellow, Unbleached Titanium
Light Brown: Burnt Sienna, Mars Yellow and Unbleached Titanium.

Add these colors to the light colors from the trees.

Pat in these colors using a #3 fan brush. Alternate light and dark and warms and cools in horizontal lines. Be careful not to let the lines be obvious. Remember that cool light colors recede and warm rich colors come forward.

BUSHES

Dab in the bushes with a #16 brush using the tree colors. Add the field colors to the bushes also. They should be a bit lighter and warmer in value than the large trees.

Add more Burnt Sienna and Raw Sienna to the bushes and weeds in the foreground. Use a small stippler and some medium to thin this paint just a little. Put in a few squiggles with a #1 liner for weed stems. Use Burnt Umber for this.

Sign and enjoy.

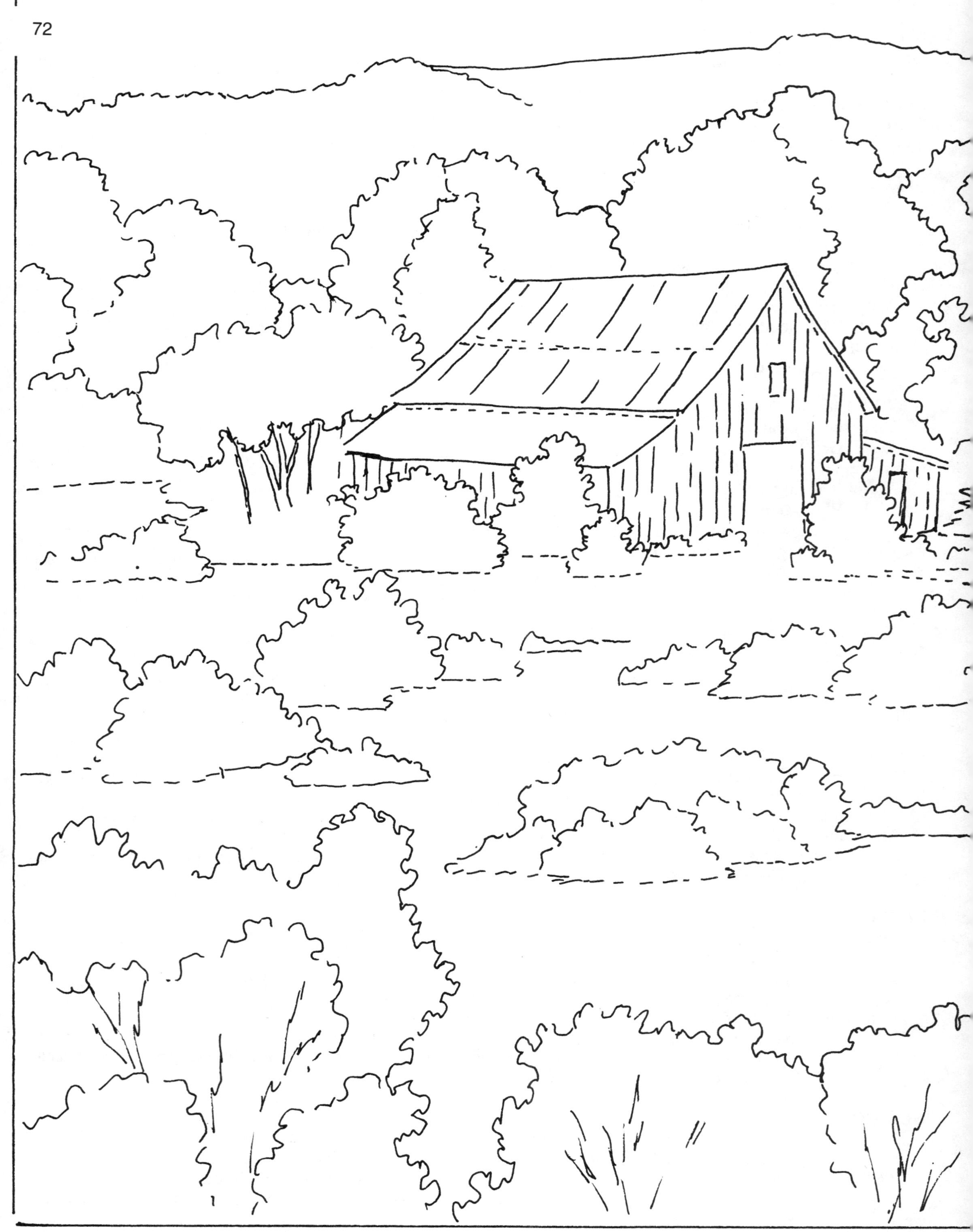

RED BARN

AFTER THE RAIN

PALETTE
White
Brilliant Yellow Light
Cadmium Yellow Light
Yellow Ochre
Green Oxide
Ultramarine Blue
Alizarine Crimson
Raw Sienna
Burnt Sienna

BRUSHES
Flat Sable #30
Fan Brush #3
Liner #3

MEDIUM: Stand Oil Light or L.O.T.

CANVAS: 16 x 20

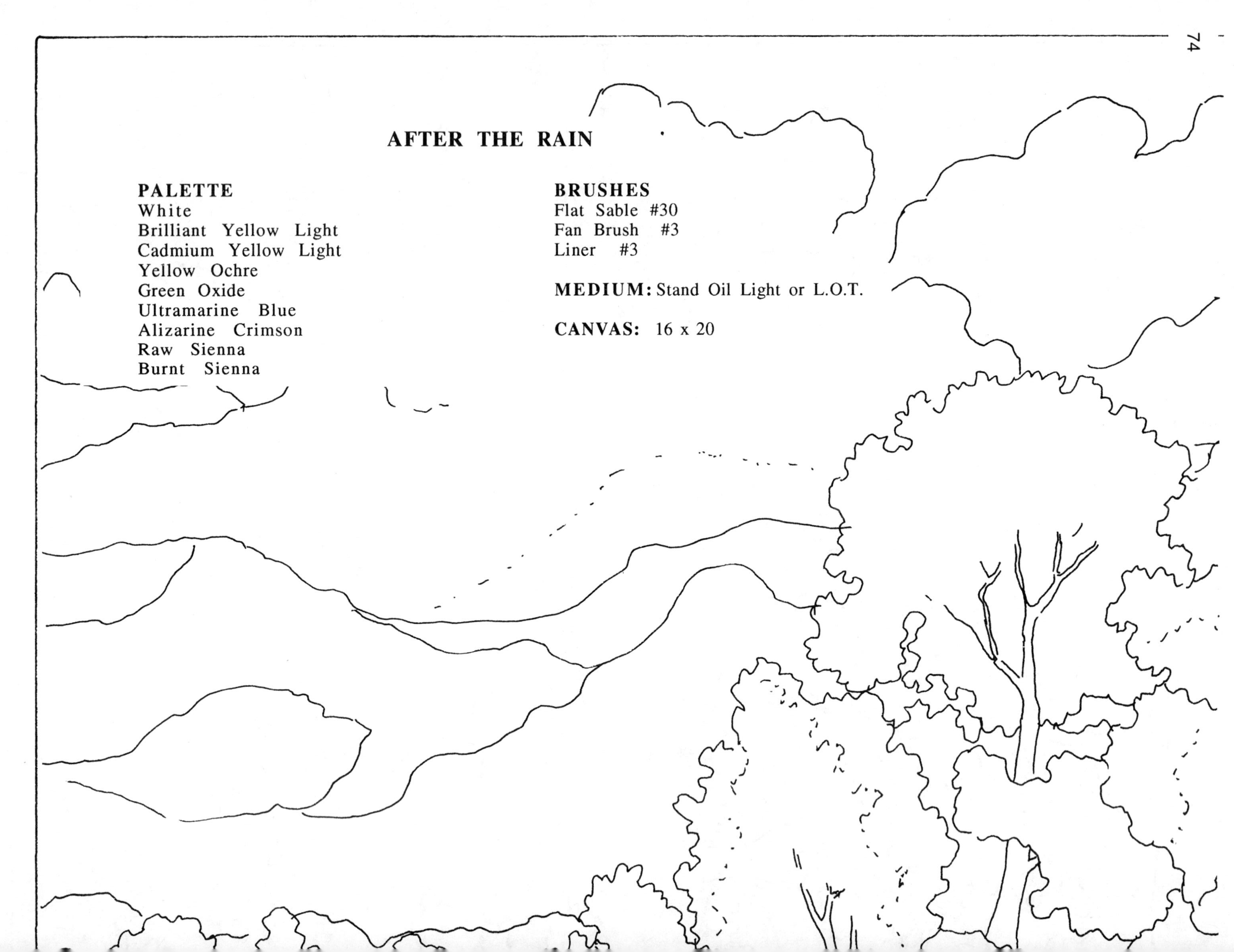

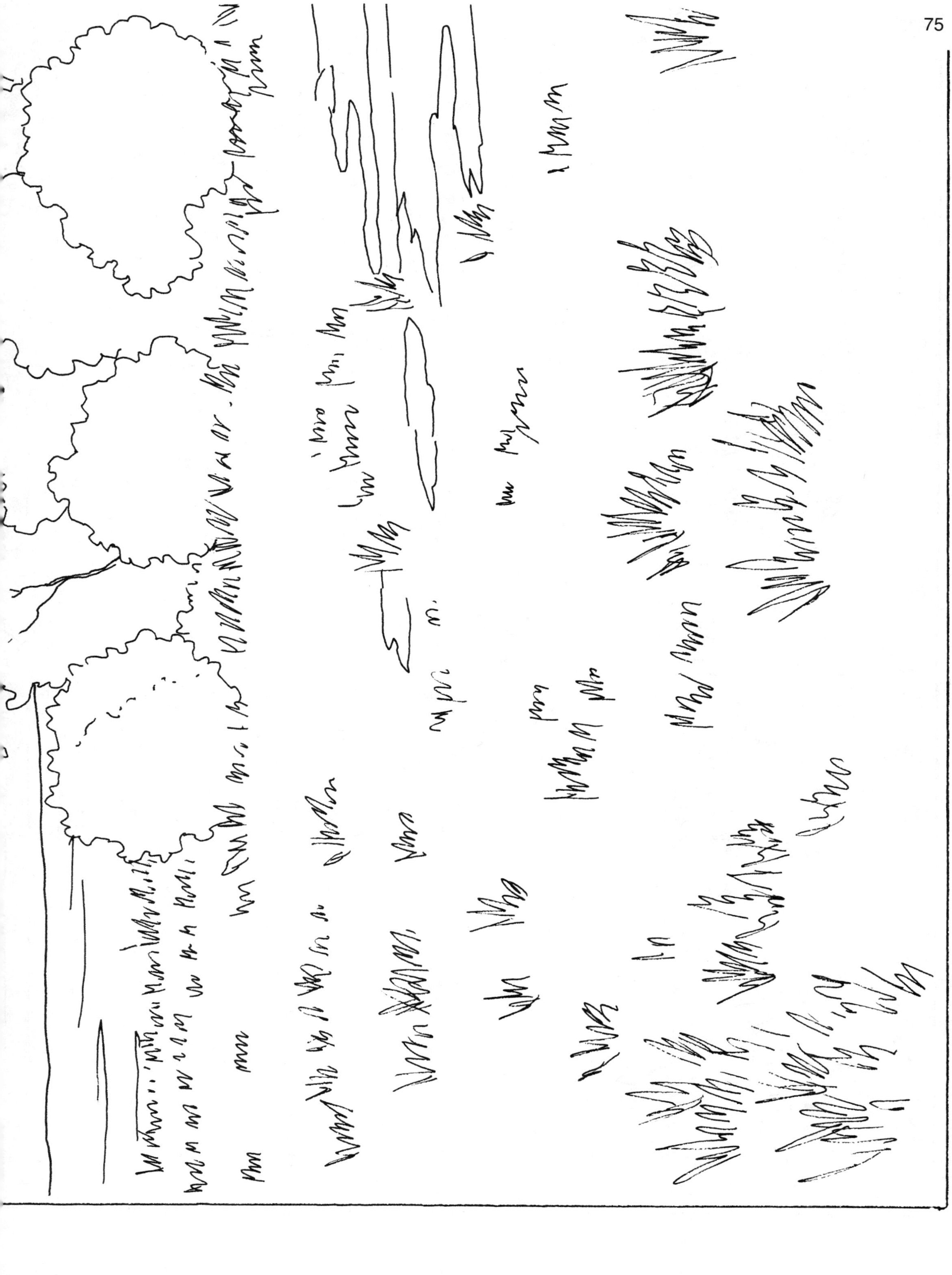

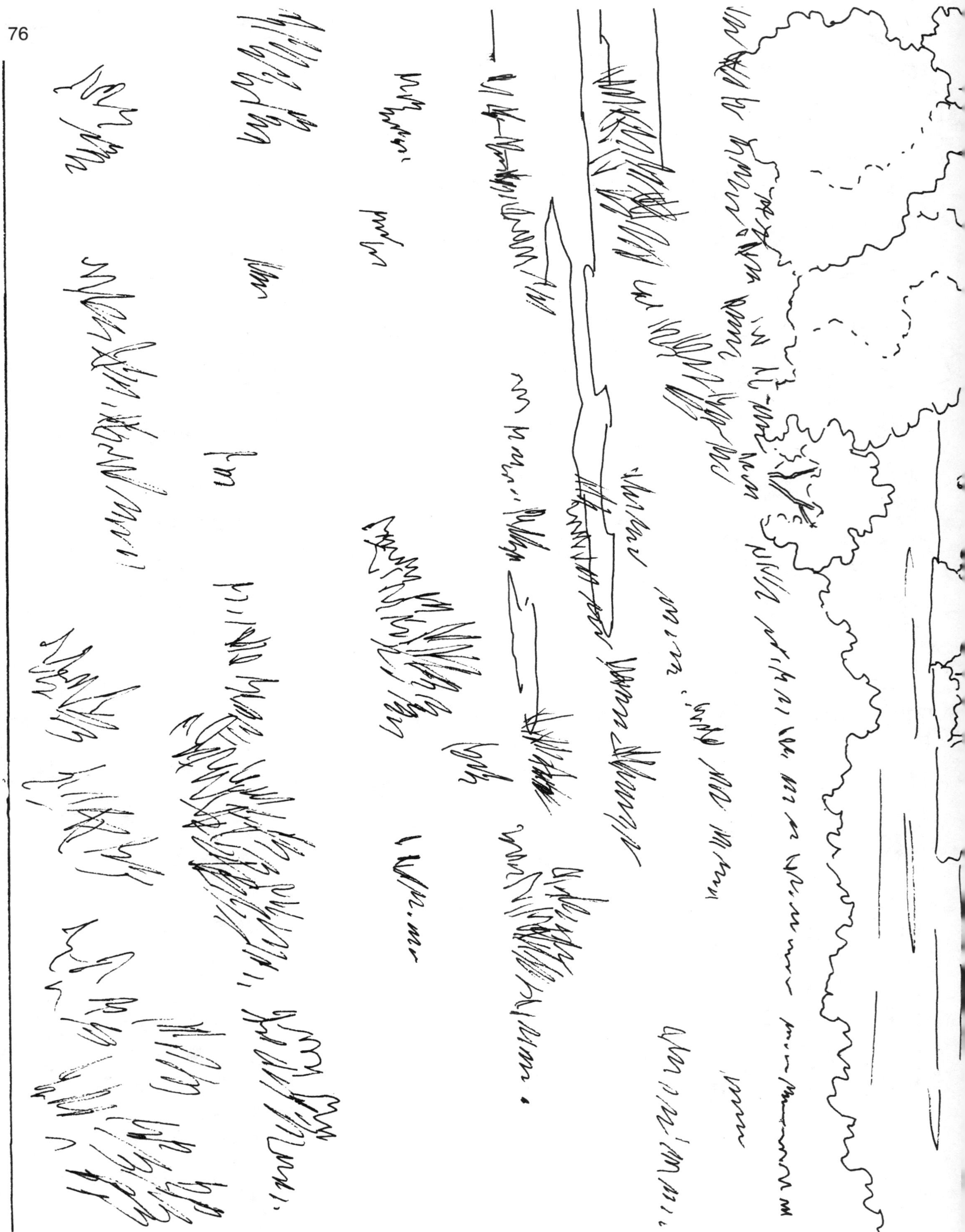

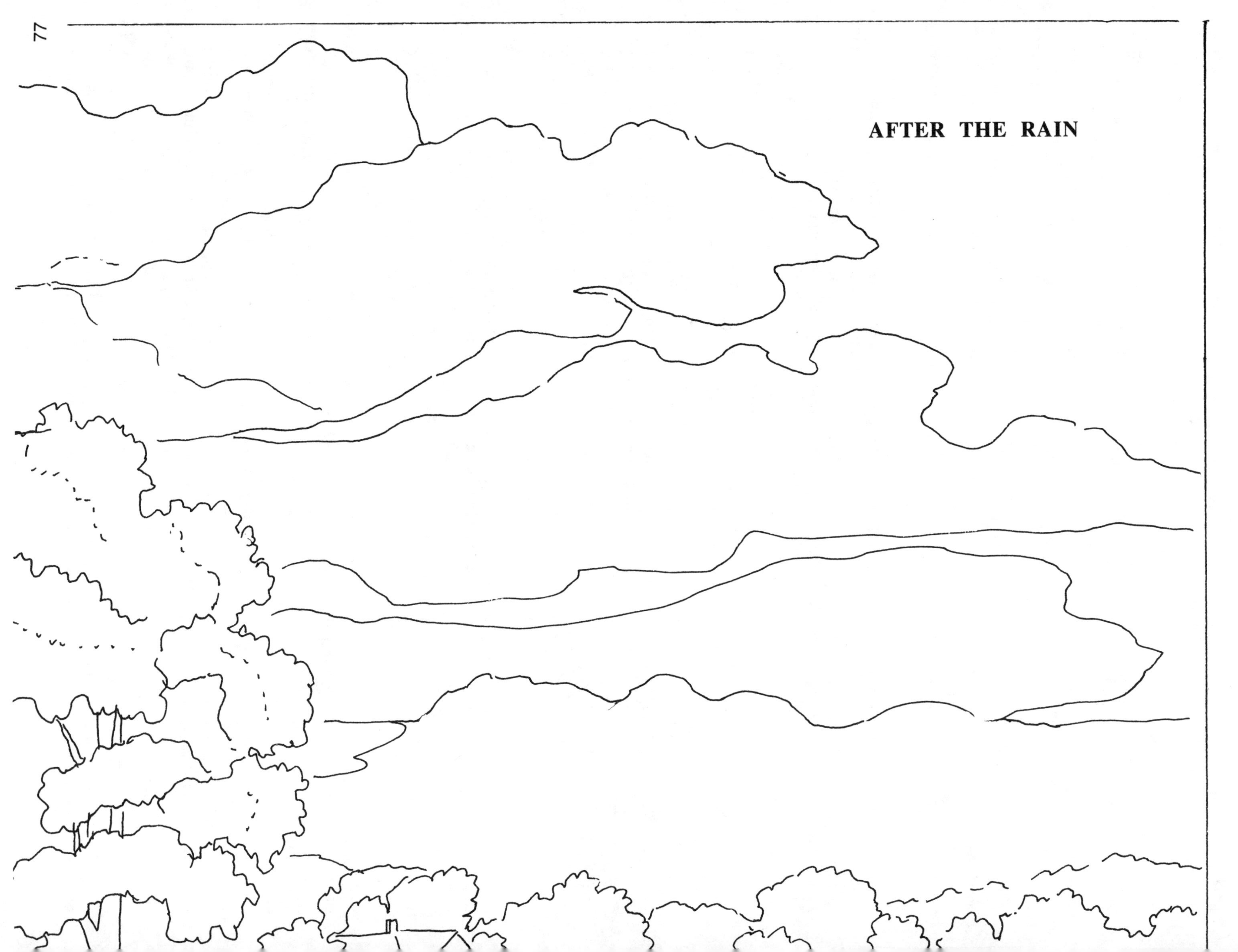

AFTER THE RAIN

AFTER THE RAIN

Prime the canvas using turpentine tinted light tan with Burnt Sienna. The lower third of the canvas should be a little darker than the top. Allow this to dry. Trace on the pattern.

SKY

Mix a light to medium blue with Ultramarine Blue and White. Cover the top area of the sky using a #32 flat sable brush Use very little medium.

Add a bit of Cadmium Yellow Light and more White to the blue for the blue of the lower sky.

Cover the clouds with White. Use a #8 brush and a circular motion to soften the edges into the blue.

Add some Alizarin Crimson to the blue to make a soft warm lavender. Use this for shadows on the clouds. For the sunny highlights add a bit of Brilliant Yellow Light.

BACKGROUND - TREES AND FIELD

Use a #16 flat brush to dab in the far distant trees. The blue and lavender from the sky will be good for this step.

Mix the following:

Light Green: Green Oxide and White

Light Yellow: Yellow Ochre and White

Dab in the trees in front of the blue lavender ones using these colors.

Use these colors with a little more White for the distant field. Horizontal strokes with a #18 brush will be good in this area. Add a bit of medium as needed.

Put in a dab of White for the farm buildings. Mix Burnt Sienna, Yellow Ochre and White for the roofs. Use a #4 brush for this.

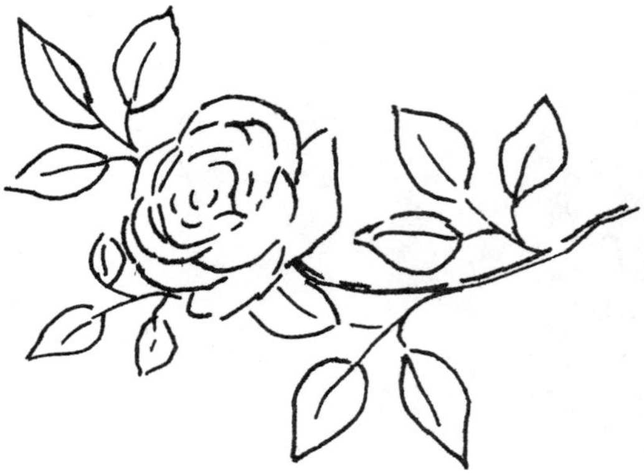

LARGE TREE AND FOREGROUND

Mix the following colors:

Dark Cool Green: Green Oxide, Ultramarine Blue and White

Medium Cool Green: The above with more White

Dark Blue: Ultramarine Blue, Green Oxide and White

Dark Warm Green: Green Oxide, Burnt Sienna and Whit

Dark Brown: Burnt Sienna, Ultramarine Blue

Dark Yellow: Cadmium Yellow Light, Burnt Sienna

Warm Yellow: Yellow Ochre, Raw Sienna, White

Warm Brown: Raw Sienna and Burnt Sienna

TREES

Use the corner of a #18 flat brush to dab in the medium cool green for the outer edge of the left side of the trees. Dab in some dark cool green for shadows. See the color illustration.

At the bottom of the tree and bush area dab in dark blue and dark brown. Leave some open spaces for light through the trees. On the warm light side of the trees dab dark yellow and medium green. Add light yellow for highlights.

Use the dark brown for the trunks and limbs. A #4 and #2 flat brush will be needed for narrow strokes.

FOREGROUND

Starting at the edge of the middle ground pat in medium cool green. Using a #3 fan brush or an old bushed out flat put some dark blue on the left side for the shadows of the trees. Add some dark brown at the base of the tree group

GRASS

Pat in horizontal lines of grass. Make these horizontal lines uneven and loose so that the ground work looks relaxed and natural. Alternate dark and lights moving towards the darker, richer colors in the bottom foreground.

Add some detailed clumps of grass at the bottom. Use a #3 liner. Thin the paint with turpentine so the liner will carry it. Dab in a few bushes.

WATER

Add the water using the sky colors. A #16 flat brush and vertical strokes are necessary for the first step. The brush gently back and forth horizontally to give the puddles a mirrored look. Sign and enjoy.

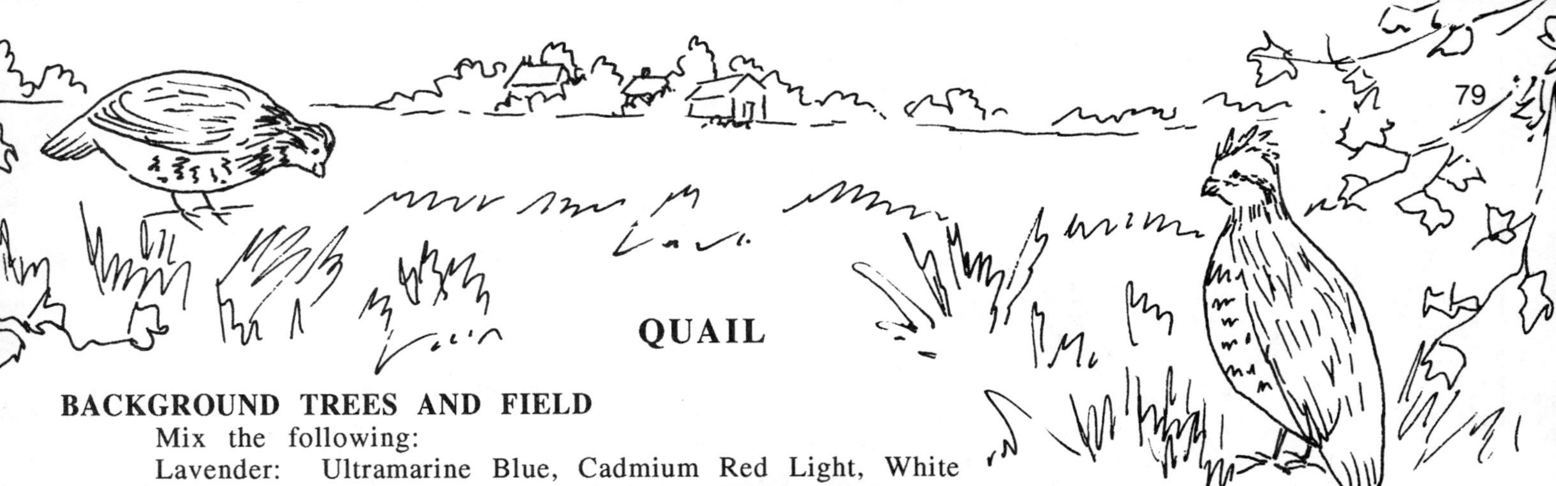

QUAIL

BACKGROUND TREES AND FIELD

Mix the following:
Lavender: Ultramarine Blue, Cadmium Red Light, White
Orange: Cadmium Red Light, Cadmium Yellow Light
Yellow: Cadmium Yellow Light, White
Tan: Raw Sienna and White

Use a #22 flat brush to put in the lavender at the bottom and right side of the trees. Dab in the other colors, moving from tan on the right to orange, to yellow on the left. Overlap each color.

Begin the field with light yellow adding the other tree colors as you move down the canvas. Pat in the colors with a #1 fan brush or the edge of a #22 flat. Use some medium.

FALLEN TREE BRANCH AND VINES

BARK - Mix the following colors:
Medium Gray: Black and White
Medium Brown: Burnt Umber and White

Use a #18 flat brush to put in the gray and brown colors. Make short streaks of color. Add some Raw Sienna for warmth and some small streaks of White for lights.

Use a #1 liner to put in the vine with medium brown. Thin this color with turpentine to an almost liquid consistency so that the liner will carry it. Mix the following leaf colors:
Red: Cadmium Red Light, Burnt Sienna
Warm Brown: Burnt Sienna and White

The leaves are casual and unformed. Pull the strokes toward the leaf center. Add some of the tree colors for sparkle.

GRASS

The foreground grass is done with all the colors previously mixed. Use the edge of a #16 flat to make vertical strokes. Make the more detailed grasses with a #1 liner. Add more Burnt Umber in the shadow under the quail.

QUAIL

These quail are impressionistic with very little detail.

Paint on the basic body colors using a #22 flat brush.

Start with the dark colors on the backs. Use overlapping strokes in dark browns. (Burnt Sienna and Burnt Umber). Then add Raw Sienna and Yellow Ochre to the middle area. On the male use White and gray for the breast area. On the hen use light tan on the breast.

Use short streaks with the flat of a #4 flat brush. Start at the tail and move upward toward the head. This give you a natural overlap of one feather over another.

Once the basic body colors are on the birds, add a few darks and lights to create the impression of detail.

Paint the males face using a #4 flat brush. Add streaks of Burnt Umber and Burnt Sienna for his crest. Put in a little Black eye. Use a #2 flat for small details. Add a White dot with a #1 spotter for the highlight in the eye.

Do the Black squiggles on the breast with a #2 flat brush. If the basic color is dry add a tiny bit of White to the Black to lighten it a little.

The feathers are not totally accurate but will give the impression of a "Bob White". Unless you want an anatomic study this will "say quail".

The feet and legs of the quail are pinkish brown. Mix Burnt Sienna, Cadmium Red Light and White for this color. Add a tiny bit of Burnt Umber for shadows.

Beaks are Black but must be painted with some brown and gray added for highlights since they have a slight shine.

Sign and enjoy.

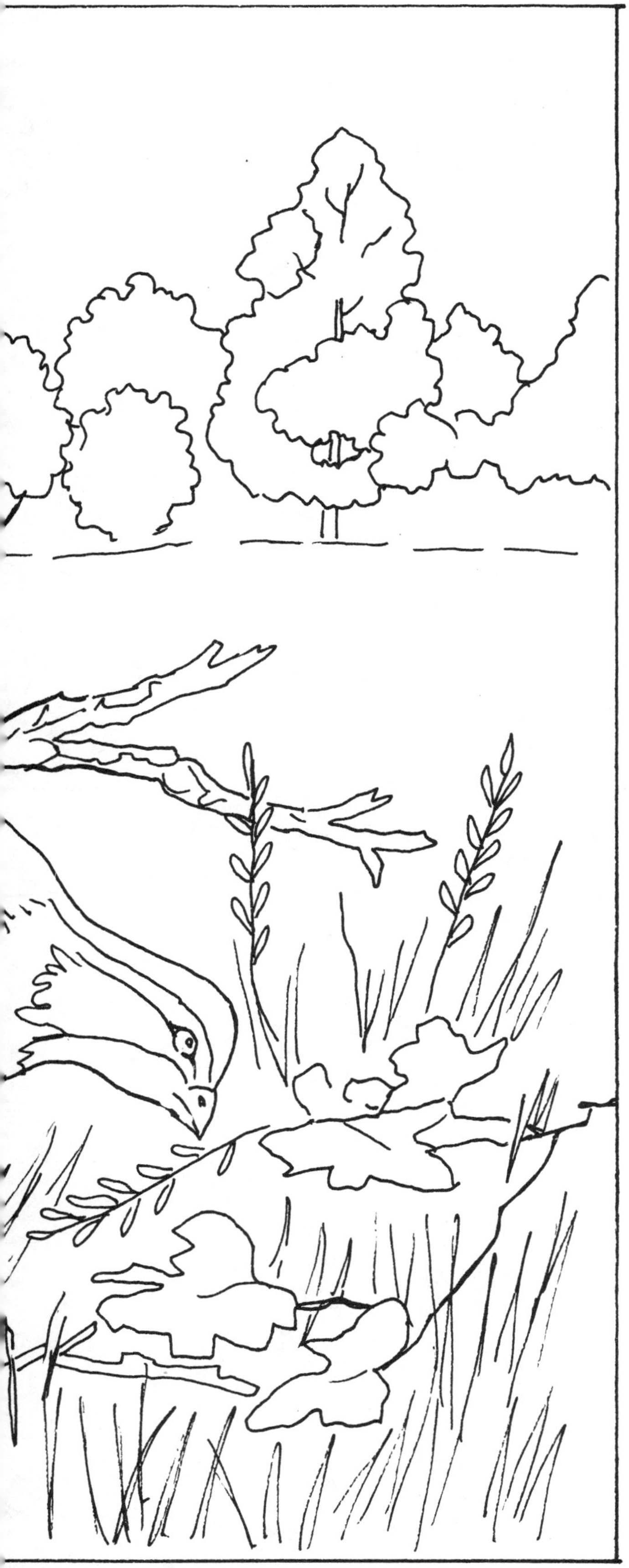

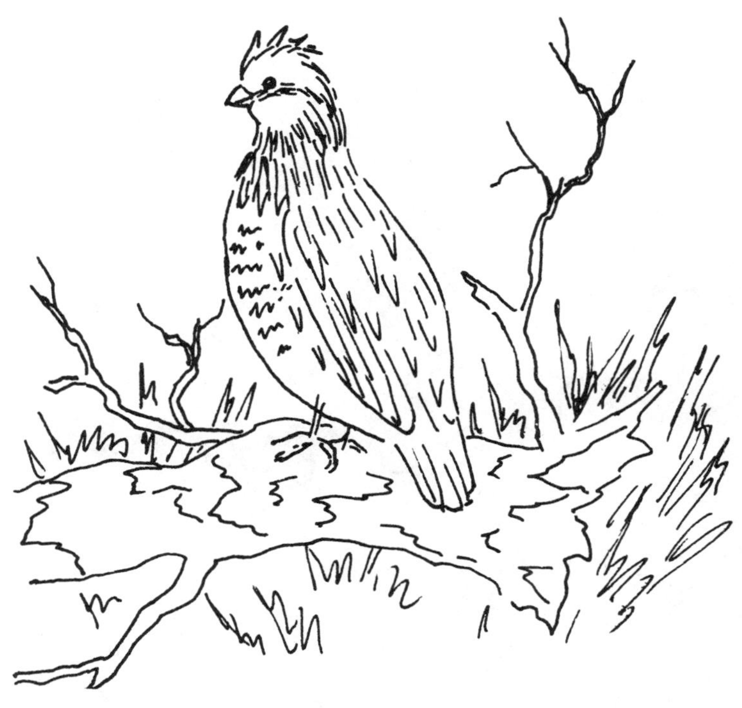

QUAIL

PALETTE
White
Yellow Ochre
Cadmium Yellow Light
Cadmium Red Light
Raw Sienna
Burnt Sienna
Burnt Umber
Ultramarine Blue
Black

BRUSHES
Flat Sables #28, 22, 26, 4, 2
Bristle Fan Brush #1
Liner #1
Spotter #1

MEDIUM Stand Oil Light or L.O.T.
Turpentine

CANVAS: 9 x 12

Prime the bottom 2/3's of the canvas with turpentine tinted to a light brown. Allow it to dry. Trace on the pattern.

SKY

Mix White and Yellow Ochre to make a pale yellow. With a #28 flat brush apply it with crisscross strokes. A small amount of medium may be used.

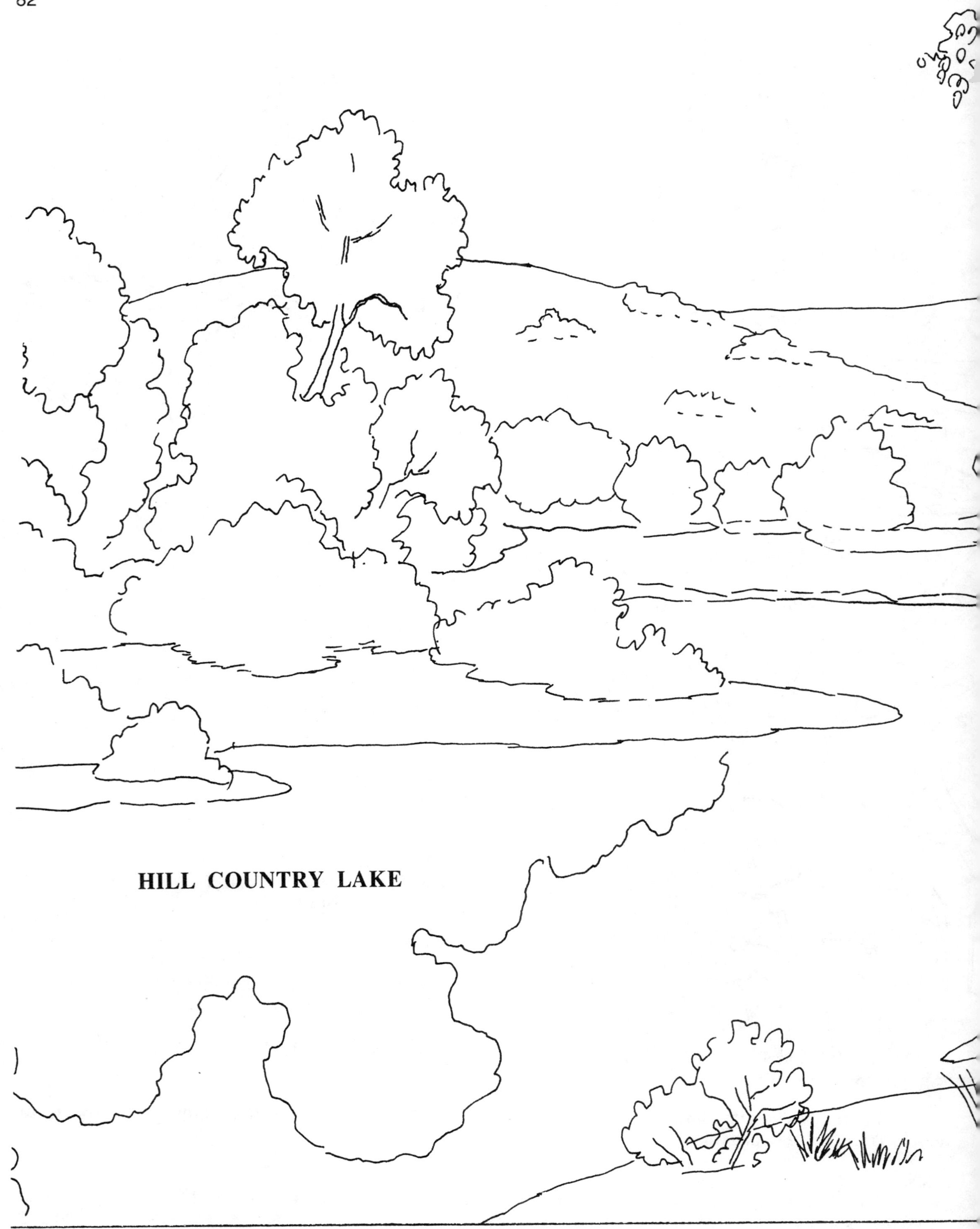

HILL COUNTRY LAKE

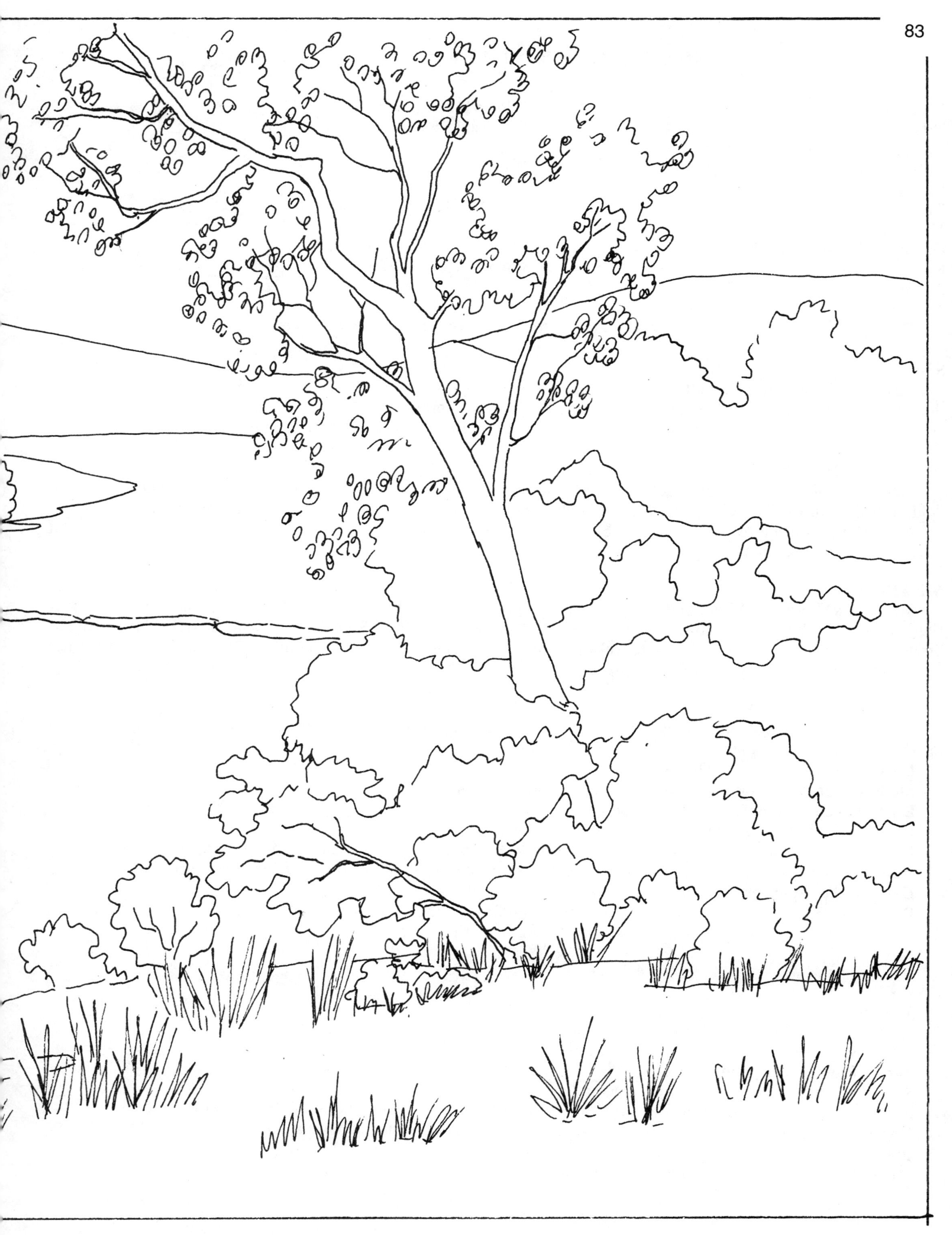

HILL COUNTRY LAKE

PALETTE
Titanium White
Parchment
Cobalt Blue
Sap Green
Raw Umber
Mars Yellow
Cadmium Yellow Light
Raw Sienna
Burnt Sienna

BRUSHES
Flat Sable #32, 18, 16, 4, 2
Liner #2
Blender - medium size

MEDIUM Stand Oil or L.O.T.
Turpentine for brush wash

CANVAS: 10 x 20

Trace the pattern on the canvas omitting the tall tree on the right side.

SKY

Mix Parchment and Cobalt Blue to make a very light blue. Paint the corners and a line across the top of the sky. Fill in the remaining sky with Parchment and blend the two colors together. Use a #32 flat brush and crisscross strokes. Some medium will be necessary.

DISTANT HILLS

Mix a medium blue from Cobalt Blue and Parchment. Use a #32 flat brush to cover this area. Add a little bit of Sap Green to the medium blue for the distant hill at the center left.

Add a tiny bit more green to the blue green mix to make the trees. Dab them on the a #16 flat brush. Use the corner of the brush.

MEADOW

Mix Mars Yellow, White and Sap Green to make a soft yellow green. Cover this area using a #32 flat brush and horizontal strokes. Mix Mars Yellow and Raw Sienna to make a rich dark yellow. Streak a little of this into the wet yellow green to create more horizontals. Dab in the small trees near the center using as #16 flat brush.

TREES

Dab in the background trees on the right with the center hill colors. Use a #16 or #18 flat brush for this.

Dark Cool Green: Sap Green, Cobalt Blue
Medium Green: Sap Green, Raw Umber and Parchment
Light Green: Sap Green, Mars Yellow
Light Yellow: Cadmium Yellow Light and White

Use #18 flat brush to crisscross in the dark green areas. See the color illustrations.

Add the medium green with a #16 flat brush. Dab this color overlapping the dark green.

Dab in the light green at the tips of the trees and bushes.

Put in some Raw Sienna to relieve and compliment the greens. Add the small tree trunks with dark brown made from Raw Umber softened with a little bit of White. Use a #2 flat brush.

EARTH

Mix the following:
Medium Cool Brown: Burnt Sienna, Cobalt Blue and White
Warm Light Brown: Burnt Sienna and White
Tan: Raw Sienna and White

See the color illustration for placement.

Put in a bit of warm light brown along the back edge of the lake and on the left side shore line. Use horizontal strokes with a #16 flat sable brush. Add some medium cool brown on the left for shadows and at the front bottom right side.

Work the edges of the green and browns together.

WATER

Cover the water area using a #32 flat brush with the sky and tree colors. Use vertical strokes and a bit more medium than usual.

Blend the whole area gently with a #32 flat or a medium size soft blender. Add tiny streaks of White along the back edge of the water and some on the middle right shore.

After a drying period put in the tall tree on the right. If the canvas is completely dry you can trace on the pattern. If not dry do it freehand.

Use a #2 liner and #4 and #2 flats. Mix a little White in some Burnt Umber for the dark side.

Use the light earth colors for highlights.

When using a liner thin the paint to a liquid consistency so that the liner will carry the paint.

Dab in the leaves with a #4 flat brush using the blue green hill colors and light yellow for highlights. The overlap of these colors will create middle tones.

Use the #4 flat to put in the grasses. Vertical strokes will do for the basic grass. Smooth the brush to a knife edge before starting. Use the #2 liner to add the detail grasses and your are finished.

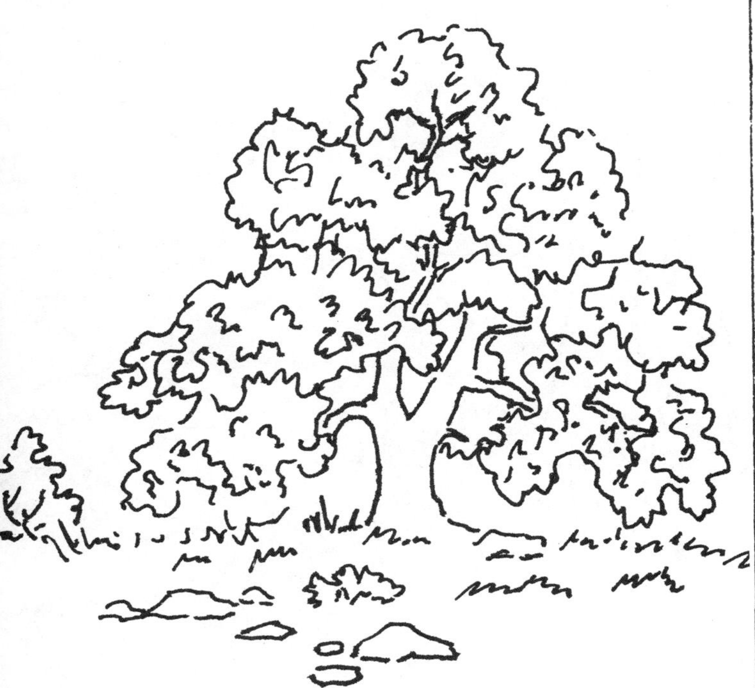

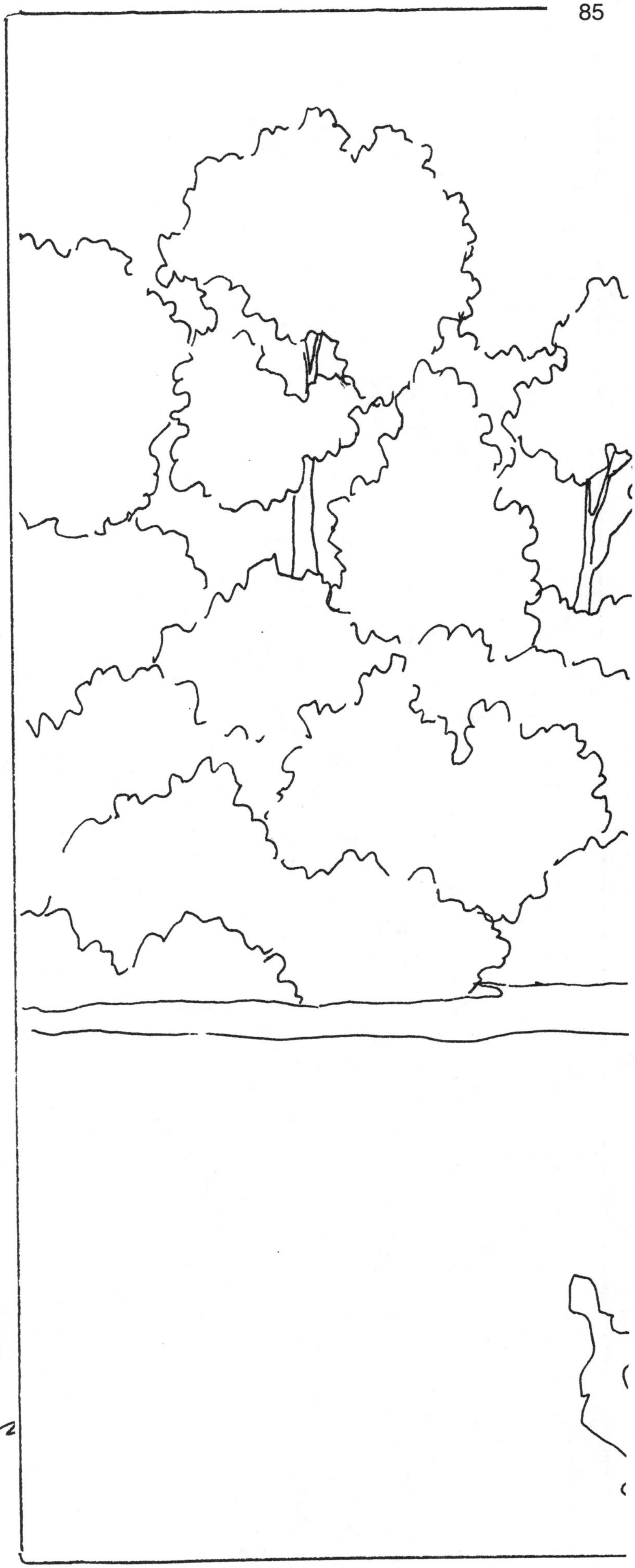

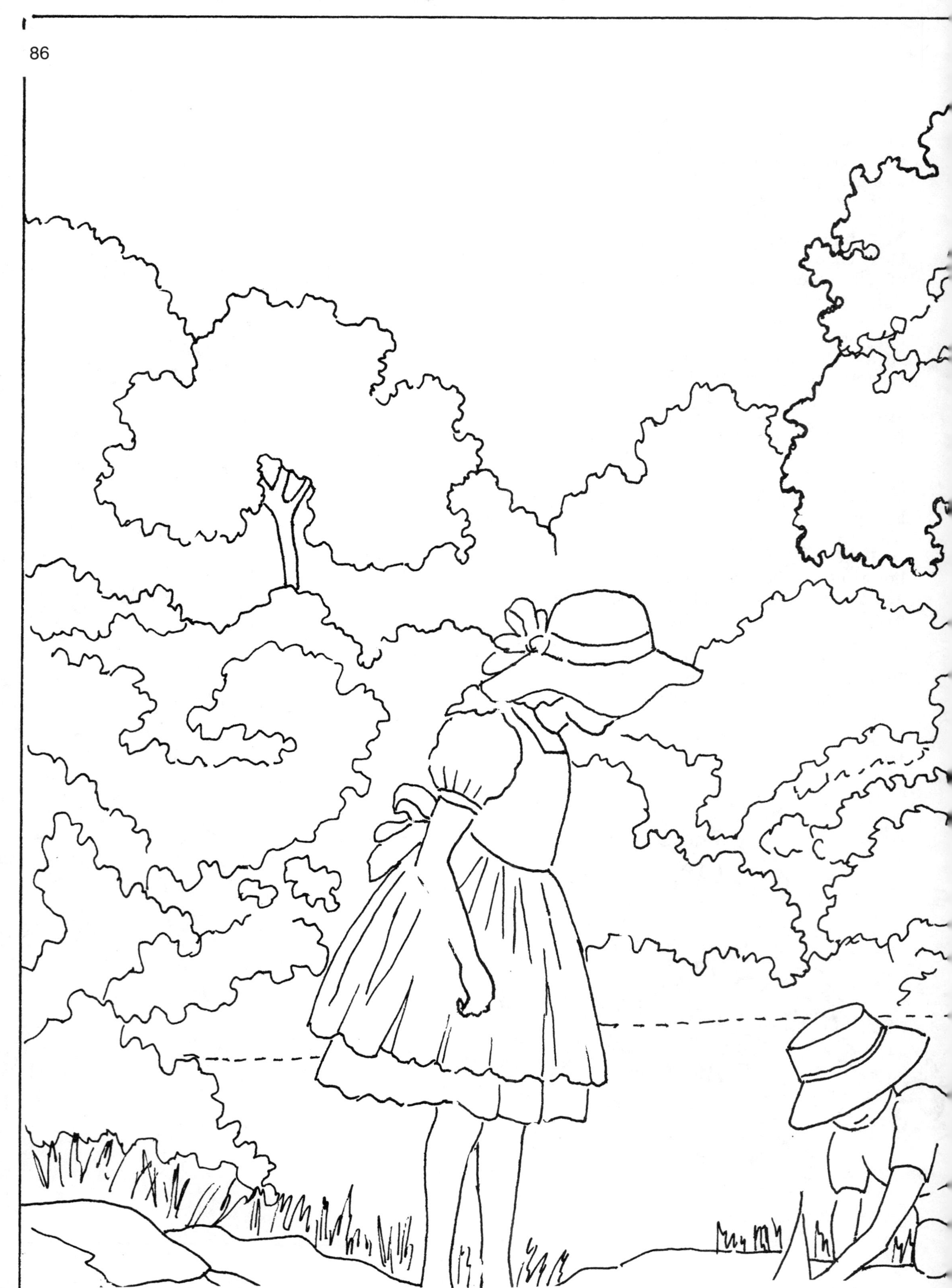

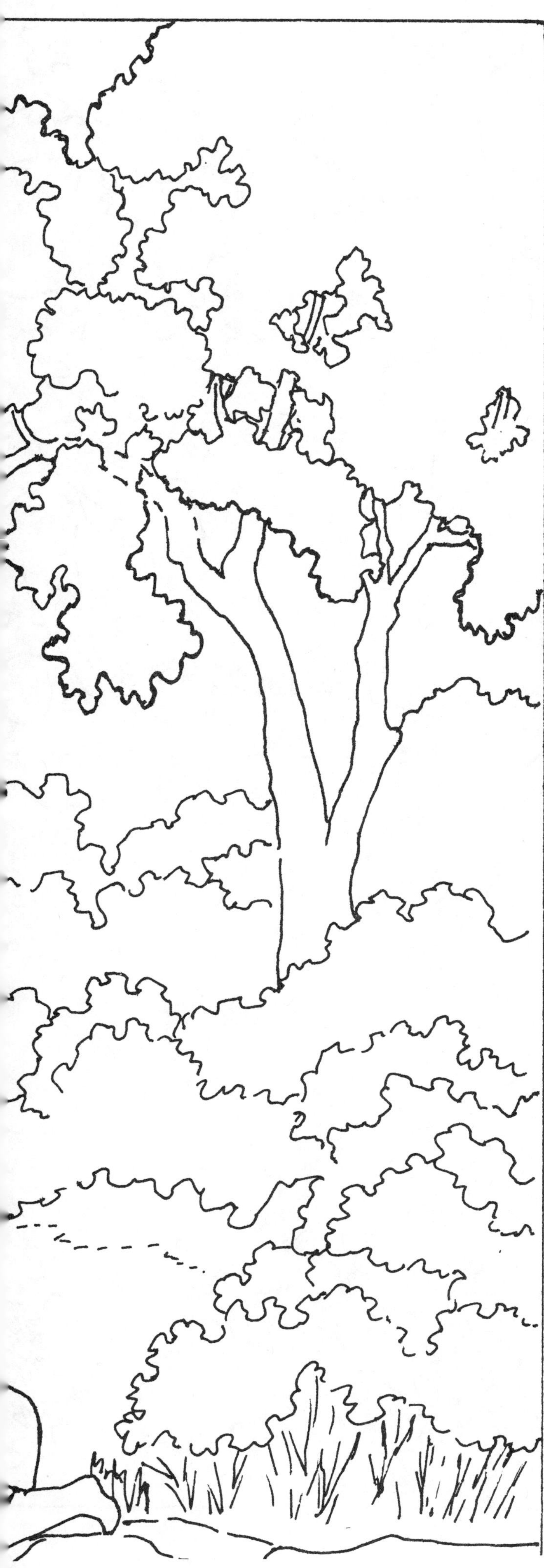

CHILDREN AND THE BOAT

BRUSHES
Flat Sable #32, 28, 18, 16, 4, 2
Blender Medium Size

MEDIUM Stand Oil Light or L.O.T.

CANVAS: 12 x 16

PALETTE
White
Cadmium Yellow Light
Cobalt Blue
Sap Green
Yellow Ochre
Cadmium Red Light
Raw Umber
Alizarine Crimson

Trace the pattern on the canvas.

SKY

Mix a light blue from Cobalt Blue and White. Use a #32 flat brush to crisscross in the sky with this color. Paint well into the edge of the trees.

TREES

Mix the following:
Medium Green: Sap Green, Cobalt Blue and White
Light Green: Add more White to medium green.
Pale Green: Add more White to light green.
Yellow Green: Add Cadmium Yellow Light to medium green.

For the distant trees use the pale green. Dab in this color with a #18 flat brush.

Use the light green for the next layer of trees. Continue to dab.

For the large tree,use the medium green for a basic color. Dab in the yellow green for lights. Use medium as necessary.

The tree trunk is done with Raw Umber lightened with White. It will be highlighted with pink and yellow flower colors while the brown is wet. Use vertical strokes with a #16 flat brush. A #4 will be good for the small limbs.

Prime the area behind the flowers with turpentine tinted to medium green with Sap Green. Allow to dry or set up before you start the flowers.

Mix the following:
Pink: Alizarine Crimson, White
Warm Pink: Cadmium Red Light and White
Lavender: Alizarine Crimson, Cobalt Blue and White
Yellow: Cadmium Yellow Light, Cadmium Red Light and White

Dab in the flower colors with the corner of a #16 flat brush. Vary the colors by adding White.

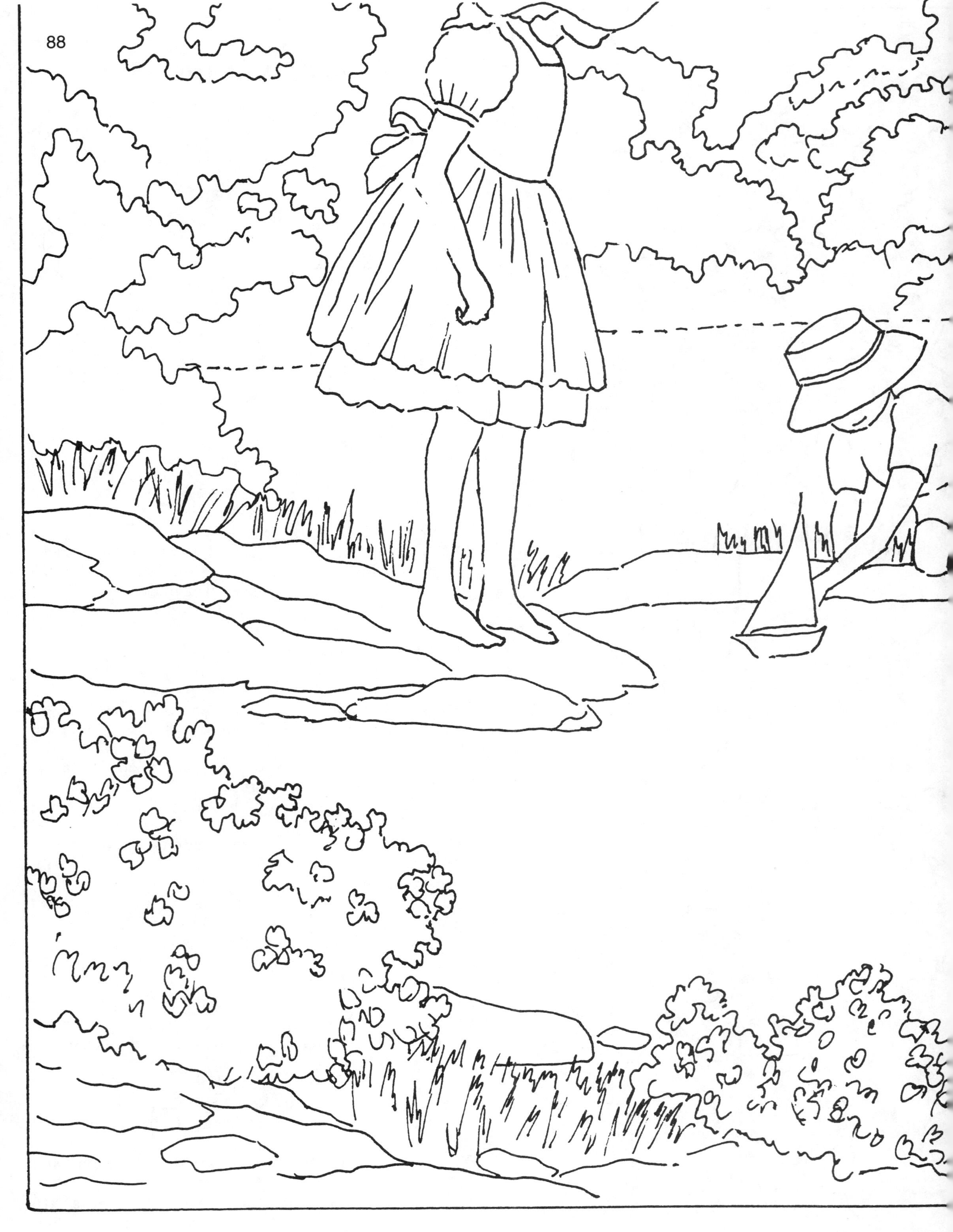

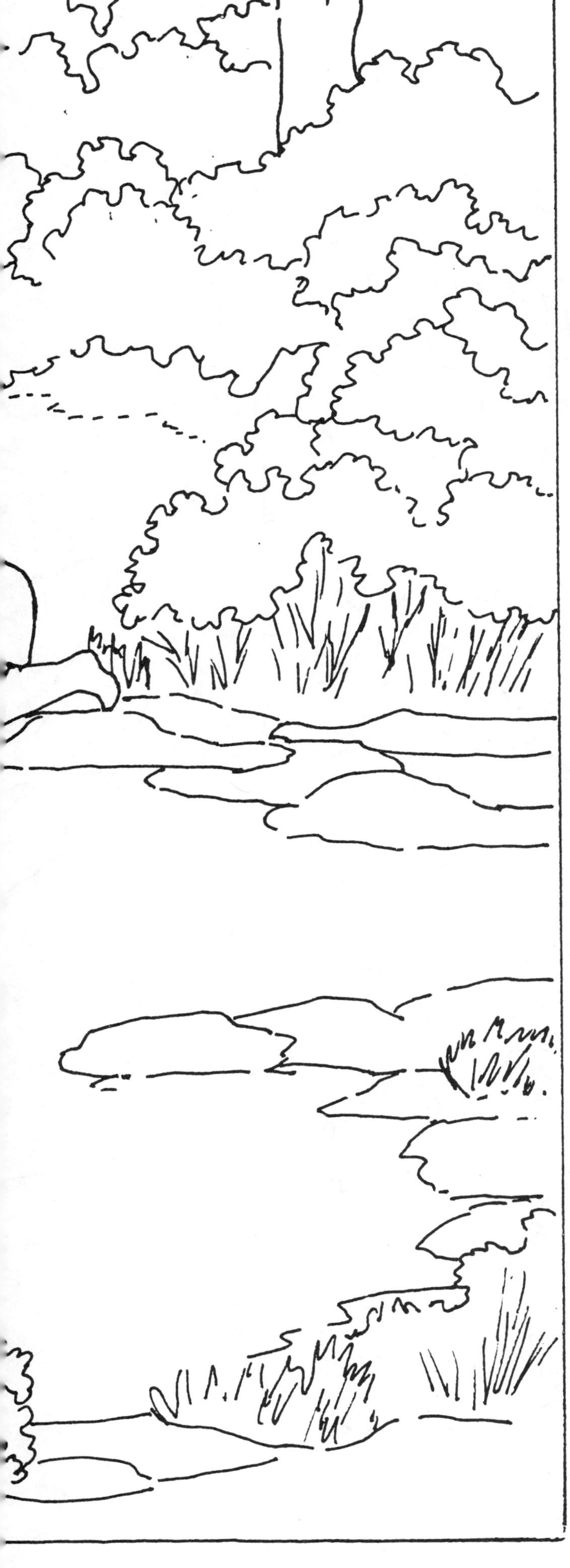

Continue to use the greens for flowers and plants.

LAWN

Use some of the light green, from the trees, at the back of the lawn. Then begin to use more yellow greens. With a #18 flat put in the greens using horizontal strokes. Do some patting over the horizontals at the very front. Add some vertical strokes just back of the children. Mix Sap Green and White with a bit of Yellow Ochre for the richer foreground grass.

ROCKS

Mix Raw Umber and White to make a medium and a light brown. Put in the medium brown first and top it off with light. You may add bits of blue and lavender from the flowers. Put in the shadows on the rocks.

CHILDREN

Mix the following flesh colors.

Medium Flesh: Cadmium Red Light, Yellow Ochre and White.

Light Flesh: Add more White to medium flesh.

Cover the flesh areas with medium flesh. Use a #10 flat brush and a #4 and #2 flats for small parts.

Use the light flesh for highlight. Work some lavender into the shadows.

CLOTHING

PINK DRESS - Use the warm and cool pinks from the flowers on the dress. Use the cool pink on the shadow side and warm pink on the light side. Add some White highlights on the folds.

For the white clothing mix a tiny bit of Raw Umber with the blue sky color for shadows.

Generally it is best to follow the lines of clothing with the brush strokes. Use a #16 brush for large areas and the #4 and #2 brushes for smaller things.

Use the blue flower color for the boy's pants. Add a tiny bit of Raw Umber to this for the shadows.

His hat is Yellow Ochre shaded to light yellow for the highlights.

WATER

Repeat the sky color in the water with flower colors. Add in the appropriate places. See the color illustration. Put in the water with a #28 brush with vertical strokes.

Blend the colors with a medium size blender using horizontal strokes.

Use the #4 flat brush to add ripples with White. Back up these ripples with a tiny bit of light blue.

The boat is a dark red made from Cadmium Red Light and Raw Umber.

Mix some dark green from Sap Green and Raw Umber to dab in the foreground bushes. Add the lighter green for lights and some pink flowers.

Sign and enjoy.

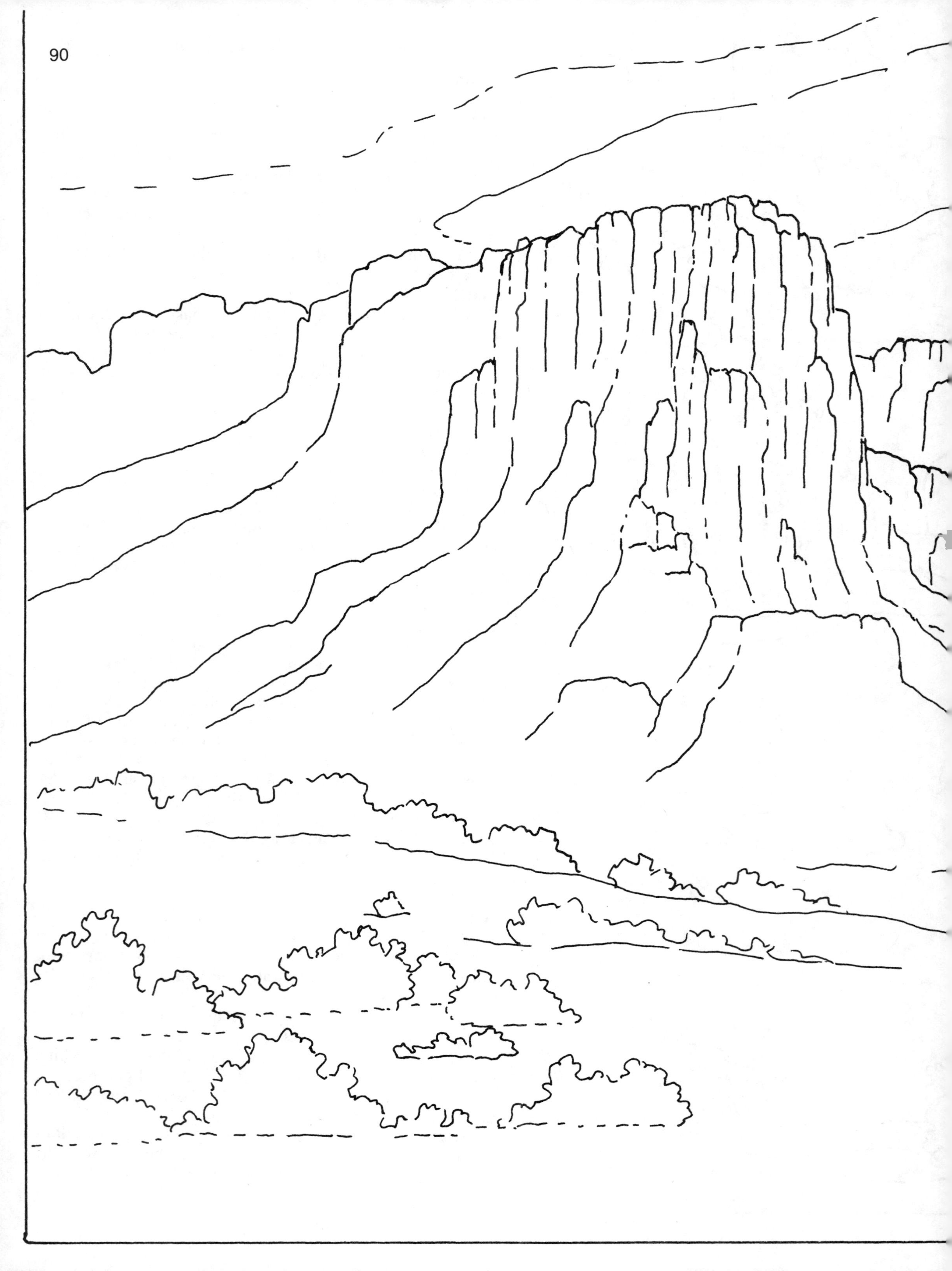

THE SHINING MOUNTAIN

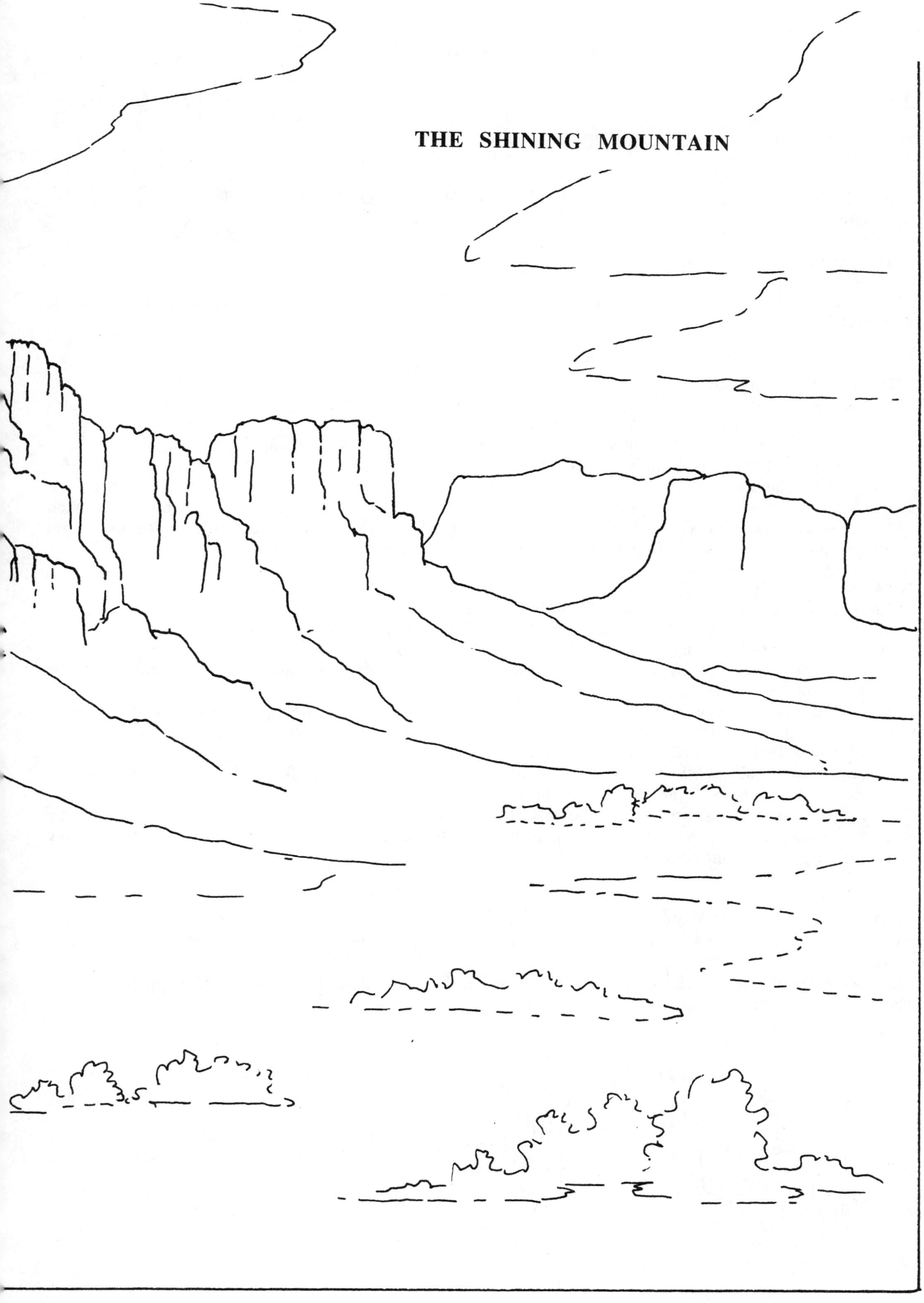

THE SHINING MOUNTAIN

PALETTE
White
Brilliant Yellow Light
Mars Yellow
Cadmium Yellow Light
Cadmium Red Light
Alizarin Crimson
Raw Umber
Ultramarine Blue

BRUSHES
Flat Sables #32, 18, 16, 4, 2
Large Blender
Stippler #2

MEDIUM Stand Oil Light or L.O.T.
Turpentine

CANVAS: 12 x 16

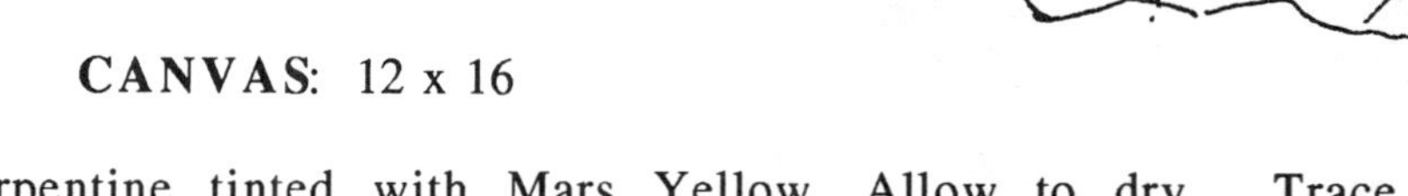

Prime the canvas by wiping with turpentine tinted with Mars Yellow. Allow to dry. Trace on the pattern.

SKY

Mix the following colors:
Cool Gray: Ultramarine Blue, Alizarine Crimson
Peach: Cadmium Red Light, Mars Yellow and White
Mauve: Same colors as the gray but add a bit more Alizarine Crimson
Pale Yellow: Cadmium Yellow Light, Mars Yellow and White

With a #32 flat sable brush put in the lightest part of the sky. A crisscross stroke is good for laying in color. Next add peach to the warm glowing areas. These are mostly on the left side. Add the dark clouds with cool gray. Allow some overlapping of color. Add some Brilliant Yellow Light to the lightest part of the sky. Blend gently with a large blender.

MOUNTAINS

Continue to use the sky colors plus the following:
Orange: Cadmium Red Light, Cadmium Yellow Light and White
Rust: Alizarine Crimson, Cadmium Yellow Light and White

Use cool gray overlaid with a bit of peach for the distant mountain. A #18 brush will be good for these smaller areas.

Put in the deep shadow areas in the foreground mountain using cool gray. Add a bit of Raw Umber for the darkest parts. Moving toward the right side of the canvas the shadows become lighter. Add some Brilliant Yellow Light to the gray and peach.

Use some rust and peach in the front shadows to bring this area forward. Cover the lightest areas with peach and bits of orange. Begin to use vertical strokes.

Once the basic colors are done, the details will be added with a #4 flat brush. Vary the shadow colors using cool gray and rust toned down with peach. Use light yellow (from the sky colors) to highlight the mountains.

FOREGROUND

Mix Raw Umber and White to make a medium brown. Use this color plus the sky colors for the ground. A #32 brush with horizontal strokes cause the ground to be flat. See the illustration for color placement.

Mix Raw Umber and a bit of Mars Yellow for the bushes. Add these with a #2 stippler.

Now you are finished.

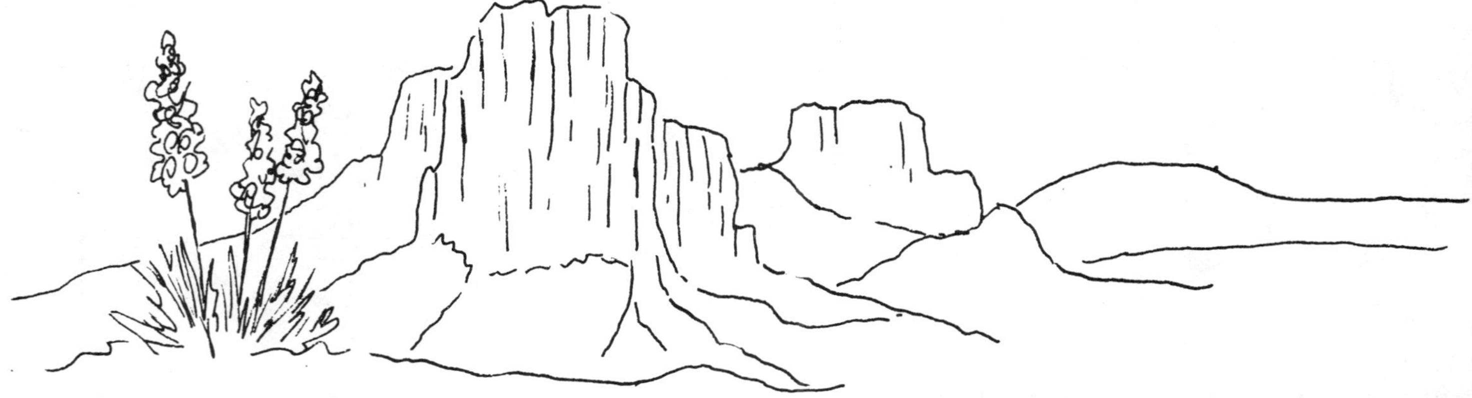

SHIPPING & HANDLING CHARGES

****

Add $1.75 for the First Book for shipping and handling.

Add $1.25 per each additional book.

Please Add $3.00 for handlin& postage, PER TAPE. Sorry we must have a "NO REFUND-NO RETURN " policy.

U.S. CURRENCY

ACRYLIC BOOKS

Vol. 1 "Love Lives Here" by Mary Lynn Lewis....170 $6.50 _____
Vol. 2 "Love Lives Here" by Mary Lynn Lewis....185 $6.50 _____
Vol. 3 "Love Lives Here" by Mary Lynn Lewis....195 $6.50 _____
Vol. 1 "Wildflower Sampler" by Bev Norman....191 $7.50 _____
Vol. 1 "Whimsical Critters" by Lori Ohlson....228 $7.50 _____
Vol. 1 "Holiday Medley" by Nina Owens....265 $7.50 _____
Vol. 1 "Oh Those Little Rascals" by Diane Permenter....247 $7.50 _____
Vol. 1 "Forever In My Heart" by Diane Richards....188 $6.50 _____
Vol. 2 "Memories In My Heart" by Diane Richards....189 $6.50 _____
Vol. 3 "Forever In My Heart II" by Diane Richards....205 $7.50 _____
Vol. 5 "Memories In Your Heart" by Diane Richards....237 $7.50 _____
Vol. 6 "Angels In My Stocking" by Diane Richards....254 $7.50 _____
Vol. 1 "Creations in Canvas...and More" by Carol Spooner....256 $7.50 _____
Vol. 1 "Rise and Shine" by Jolene Thompson....214 $6.50 _____
Vol. 2 "Garden Gate" by Jolene Thompson....250 $7.50 _____
Vol. 1 "Count Your Blessings" by Chris Thornton....176 $7.50 _____
Vol. 2 "Count Your Blessings" by Chris Thornton....180 $6.50 _____
Vol. 3 "Count Your Blessings" by Chris Thornton....196 $6.50 _____
Vol. 4 "Count Your Blessings" by Chris Thornton....206 $7.50 _____
Vol. 5 "Count Your Blessings" by Chris Thornton....213 $6.50 _____
Vol. 6 "Share Your Blessings" by Chris Thornton....226 $7.50 _____
Vol. 7 "Blessings" by Chris Thornton....255 $7.50 _____
Vol. 8 "Christmas Blessings" by Chris Thornton....266 $7.50 _____
Vol. 4 "Daydreams & Sweet Shirts" by Don & Lynn Weed....198 $7.50 _____
Vol. 5 "Daydreams & Sweet Shirts II" by Don & Lynn Weed....208 $7.50 _____
Vol. 1 "Floral Fabrics and Watercolor" by Sally Williams....262 $7.50 _____
Vol. 1 "Friendship Garden" by Shirley Wingert....253 $7.50 _____

WATERCOLOR BOOKS

Vol. 19 "Gift of Painting" by Susan Scheewe....O/AC/WC....230 $7.50 _____
Vol. 20 "Simply Country Watercolors" by Susan Scheewe....257 $7.50 _____
Vol. 21 "Simply Watercolor" by Susan Scheewe...TV Book....260 $11.95 _____
Vol. 4 "Enjoy Watercolor" by Ellie Cook....210 $7.50 _____
Vol. 5 "Celebrate The Moments With Watercolor" by Ellie Cook....227 $7.50 _____
Vol. 6 "Watercolor Memories" by Ellie Cook....246 $7.50 _____
Vol. 1 "Watercolor Made Easy" by Kathie George....190 $7.50 _____
Vol. 2 "Watercolor Made Easy" by Kathie George....236 $7.50 _____
Vol. 1 "The Way I Started" by Gary Hawk....120 $6.00 _____
Vol. 2 "Anyone Can Watercolor" by Ken Johnston....118 $6.50 _____
Vol. 3 "Anyone Can Watercolor" by Ken Johnston....119 $6.50 _____
Vol. 1 "Watercolor Fun and Easy" by Beverrly Kaiser....243 $7.50 _____
Vol. 1 "Floral Fabrics and Watercolor" by Sally Williams....262 $7.50 _____

PEN AND INK BOOKS / COLORED PENCIL BOOKS

Vol. 1 "Creative Quill" by Claudia Nice....133 $6.50 _____
Vol. 2 "Barnyards and Billygoats" by Claudia Nice....134 $6.50 _____
Vol. 3 "Wing and Wildflowers" by Claudia Nice....135 $6.50 _____
Vol. 5 "Pen and Brush Animals" by Claudia Nice....137 $6.50 _____
Vol. 6 "Journey of Memories" by Claudia Nice....166 $6.50 _____
Vol. 7 "Scenes from Seasons Past" by Claudia Nice....183 $7.50 _____
Vol. 8 "Taste of Summer" by Claudia Nice....223 $7.50 _____
Vol. 1 "Colored Pencil Made Easy" by Jane Wunder....232 $7.50 _____
Vol. 2 "Colored Pencil Made Easy" by Jane Wunder....242 $7.50 _____
Vol. 3 "The Beauty of Colored Pencil and Ink Drawing" by Jane Wunder....259 $7.50 _____

FABRIC PAINTING BOOKS

Vol. 1 "Painting It's Our Bag" by Bev Hink/Susan Scheewe....193 $7.50 _____
Vol. 2 "Painting It's Our Bag" by Bev Hink/ Susan Scheewe....209 $7.50 _____
Vol. 1 "Whimsical Critters" by Lori Ohlson....228 $7.50 _____
Vol. 1 "Oh Those Little Rascals" by Diane Permenter....247 $7.50 _____
Vol. 3 "Forever In My Heart II" by Diane Richards....205 $7.50 _____
Vol. 5 "Memories In Your Heart" by Diane Richards....237 $7.50 _____
Vol. 6 "Angels In My Stocking" by Diane Richards....254 $7.50 _____
Vol. 1 "Creations In Canvas and More" by Carol Spooner....256 $7.50 _____
Vol. 2 "Garden Gate" by Jolene Thompson....250 $7.50 _____
Vol. 5 "Count Your Blessings" by Chris Thornton....213 $6.50 _____
Vol. 6 "Share Your Blessings" by Chris Thornton....226 $7.50 _____
Vol. 4 "Daydreams and Sweet Shirts" by Don & Lynn Weed....198 $7.50 _____
Vol. 5 "Daydreams and Sweet ShirtsII" by Don & Lynn Weed....208 $7.50 _____
Vol. 1 "Floral Fabrics and Watercolor" by Sally Williams....262 $7.50 _____

OIL BOOKS

Vol.	Title	No.	Price	Qty
Vol.1	"His and Hers" by Susan Scheewe	101	$6.50	_____
Vol. 5	"So Dear To My Heart" by Susan Scheewe	105	$5.50	_____
Vol. 6	"Brushed With Elegance" by Susan Scheewe	106	$5.50	_____
Vol. 7	"Paint 'n Patch" by Susan Scheewe	107	$5.50	_____
Vol. 11	"I Love To Paint" by Susan Scheewe	111	$6.50	_____
Vol. 14	"Enjoy Painting Animals" by Susan Scheewe	114	$6.50	_____
Vol. 17	"Countryside Reflections" by Susan Scheewe	161	$6.50	_____
Vol. 18	"Mostly Landscapes" by Susan Scheewe	216	$7.50	_____
Vol. 19	"Gift of Painting" by Susan Scheewe...O/AC/WC	230	$7.50	_____
Vol. 1	"Western Images" by Becky Anthony	186	$6.50	_____
Vol. 3	"Fantasy Flowers II" by Georgia Bartlett	129	$6.50	_____
Vol. 2	"Soft Petals" by Georgia Bartlett	171	$6.50	_____
Vol. 6	"Painting Fantasy Flowers" by Georgia Bartlett	215	$7.50	_____
Vol. 1	"Painting, A Barrel of Fun" by Donna Bell	194	$6.50	_____
Vol. 2	"Painting, A Barrel of Fun" by Donna Bell	201	$7.50	_____
Vol. 3	"Barnscapes and More" by Donna Bell	218	$7.50	_____
Vol. 4	"Countryscapes" by Donna Bell	249	$7.50	_____
Vol. 5	"Painter to Painter" by Donna Bell	263	$7.50	_____
Vol. 1	"Natures Palette" by Carol Binford.....O/AC	248	$7.50	_____
Vol. 1	"Oil Painting The Easy Way" by Bill Blackman	219	$7.50	_____
Vol. 1	"Mini Mini More" by Terri and Nancy Brown	150	$6.50	_____
Vol. 2	"Mini Mini More" by Terri and Nancy Brown	151	$6.50	_____
Vol. 4	"Heritage Trails" by Terri and Nancy Brown	169	$6.50	_____
Vol. 1	"Windows of My World" by Jackie Clafin	174	$6.50	_____
Vol. 2	"Windows of My World" by Jackie Clafin	181	$7.50	_____
Vol. 3	"I'm Partial To Flowers" by Ellie Cook	157	$6.50	_____
Vol. 1	"Expressions In Oil" by Delores Egger	154	$6.50	_____
Vol. 2	"Expressions In Oil" by Delores Egger	164	$6.50	_____
Vol. 4	"Expressions In Oil" by Delores Egger	239	$7.50	_____
Vol. 1	"Victorian Days" by Gloria Gaffney	240	$7.50	_____
Vol. 2	"Days of Heaven" by Gloria Gaffney	252	$7.50	_____
Vol. 1	"Roses Are For Everyone" by Bill Huffaker	145	$7.50	_____
Vol. 3	"Nature's Beauty" by Bill Huffaker	177	$6.50	_____
Vol. 1	"Copper, Silver, Brass and Glass" by Susan Jenkins	211	$6.50	_____
Vol. 1	"Backroads of My Memory" by Geri Kisner	225	$6.50	_____
Vol. 2	"Backroads of My Memory" by Geri Kisner	245	$7.50	_____
Vol. 1	"Country's Edge" by Shirley Koenig....O/AC	179	$7.50	_____
Vol. 2	"Country's Edge" by Shirley Koenig....O/AC	212	$6.50	_____
Vol. 1	"Reflections of My World" by Pee Wee, Frankie Lanier	264	$7.50	_____
Vol. 1	"Ducks and Geese" by Jean Lyles	172	$6.50	_____
Vol. 1	"Stepping Stones" by Judy Nutter	121	$6.50	_____
Vol. 2	"Stepping Stones" by Judy Nutter	122	$6.50	_____
Vol. 1	"Rustic Charms" by Sharon Rachal	175	$6.50	_____
Vol. 2	"Rustic Charms II" by Sharon Rachal	199	$7.50	_____
Vol. 3	"Rustic Charms III" by Sharon Rachal	217	$6.50	_____
Vol. 4	"Rustic Charms IV" by Sharon Rachal	238	$7.50	_____
Vol. 5	"Rustic Charms V, Florals" by Sharon Rachal	261	$7.50	_____
Vol. 1	"Painting Flowers With Augie" by Augie Reis	152	$6.50	_____
Vol. 1	"Realistic Florals and More" by Judy Sleight	233	$7.50	_____
Vol. 1	"Soft & Misty Paintings" by Kathy Snider	204	$7.50	_____
Vol. 2	"Soft & Misty Paintings" by Kathy Snider	229	$7.50	_____
Vol. 3	"Soft & Misty Paintings" by Kathy Snider	251	$7.50	_____
Vol. 4	"Friends We've Known" by Gene Waggoner	187	$7.50	_____
Vol. 5	"Friends Are Forever" by Gene Waggoner	231	$7.50	_____
Vol. 1	"Fantasy Folk" by Don Weed	123	$6.50	_____
Vol. 1	"Something Special For Everyone" by Mildred Yeiser	158	$6.50	_____
Vol. 2	"Something Special For Everyone" by Mildred Yeiser	178	$6.50	_____
Vol. 4	"Something Special For Everyone" by Mildred Yeiser	235	$7.50	_____
Vol. 5	"Soft and Gentle Paintings" by Mildred Yeiser	268	$7.50	_____

VIDEOS

"The Gift Of Painting, Simply Watercolor"
By Susan Scheewe Brown. Guided instruction through tools and techniques for the beginning watercolorist............................$24.95

"The Gift Of Painting"
By Susan Scheewe Brown. Problems and solutions when painting oil landscapes. The video runs 90-minutes while two landscapes are completed........................$24.95

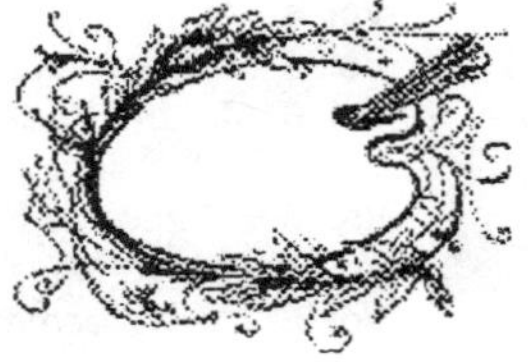

ACRYLIC BOOKS

Vol.	Title	No.	Price	Qty
Vol. 19	"Gift of Painting" by Susan Scheewe....O/AC	230	$7.50	_____
Vol. 2	"Keepsake Sampler" by Susan Scheewe/Charlene Stemple	167	$6.50	_____
Vol. 3	"Keepsake Sampler" by Susan & Camille Scheewe	173	$6.50	_____
Vol. 4	"Keepsake Sampler" by Susan & Camille Scheewe	200	$6.50	_____
Vol. 1	"Painting It's Our Bag" by Bev Hink/Susan Scheewe	193	$7.50	_____
Vol. 2	"Painting It's Our Bag" by Bev Hink/Susan Scheewe	209	$7.50	_____
Vol. 1	"Loving You" by Susan & Camille Scheewe	244	$7.50	_____
Vol. 1	"Kids and Water" by Joyce Benner	234	$7.50	_____
Vol. 1	"Natures Palette" by Carol Binford	248	$7.50	_____
Vol. 1	"Santas and Sams" by Bobi Dolora	258	$7.50	_____
Vol. 1	"Happy Heart, Happy Home" by Cathy Jones	241	$7.50	_____
Vol. 1	"Country's Edge" by Shirley Koenig......O/AC	179	$7.50	_____
Vol. 2	"Country's Edge" by Shirley Koenig......O/AC	212	$6.50	_____

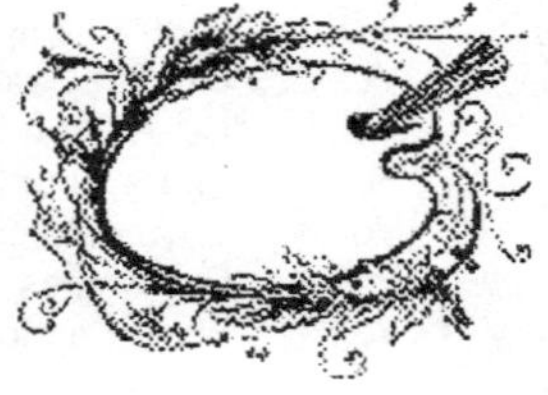

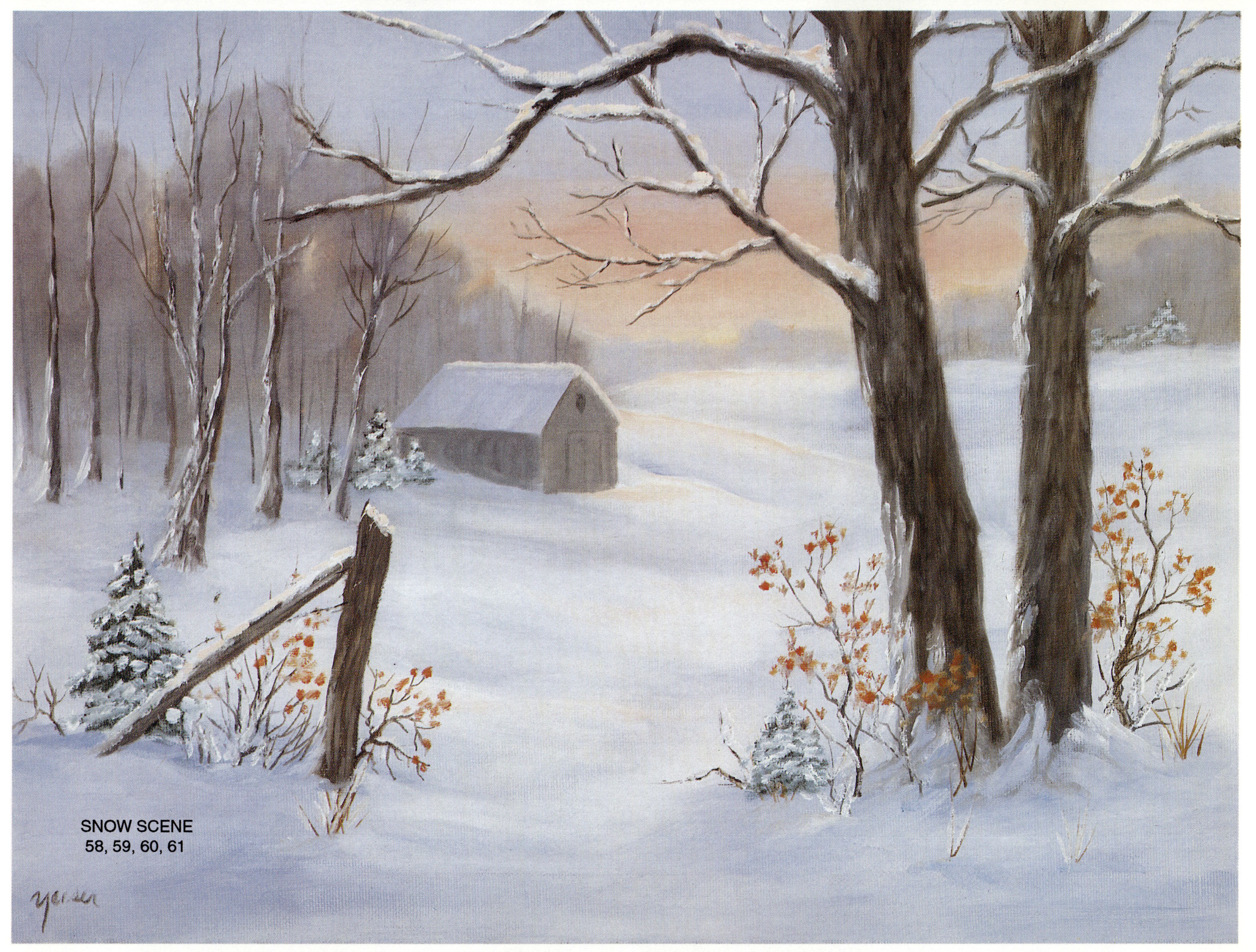

SNOW SCENE
58, 59, 60, 61

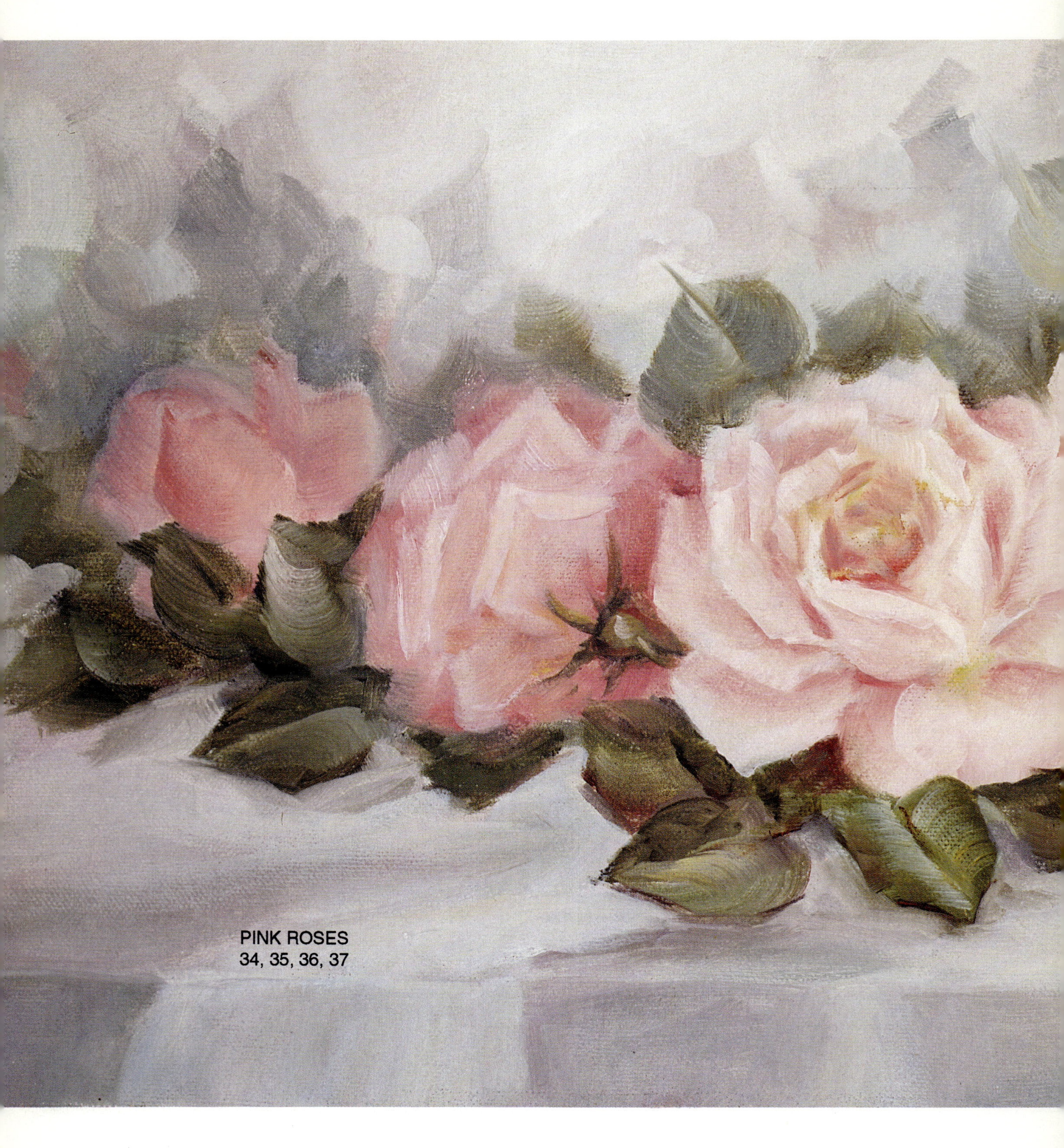

PINK ROSES
34, 35, 36, 37

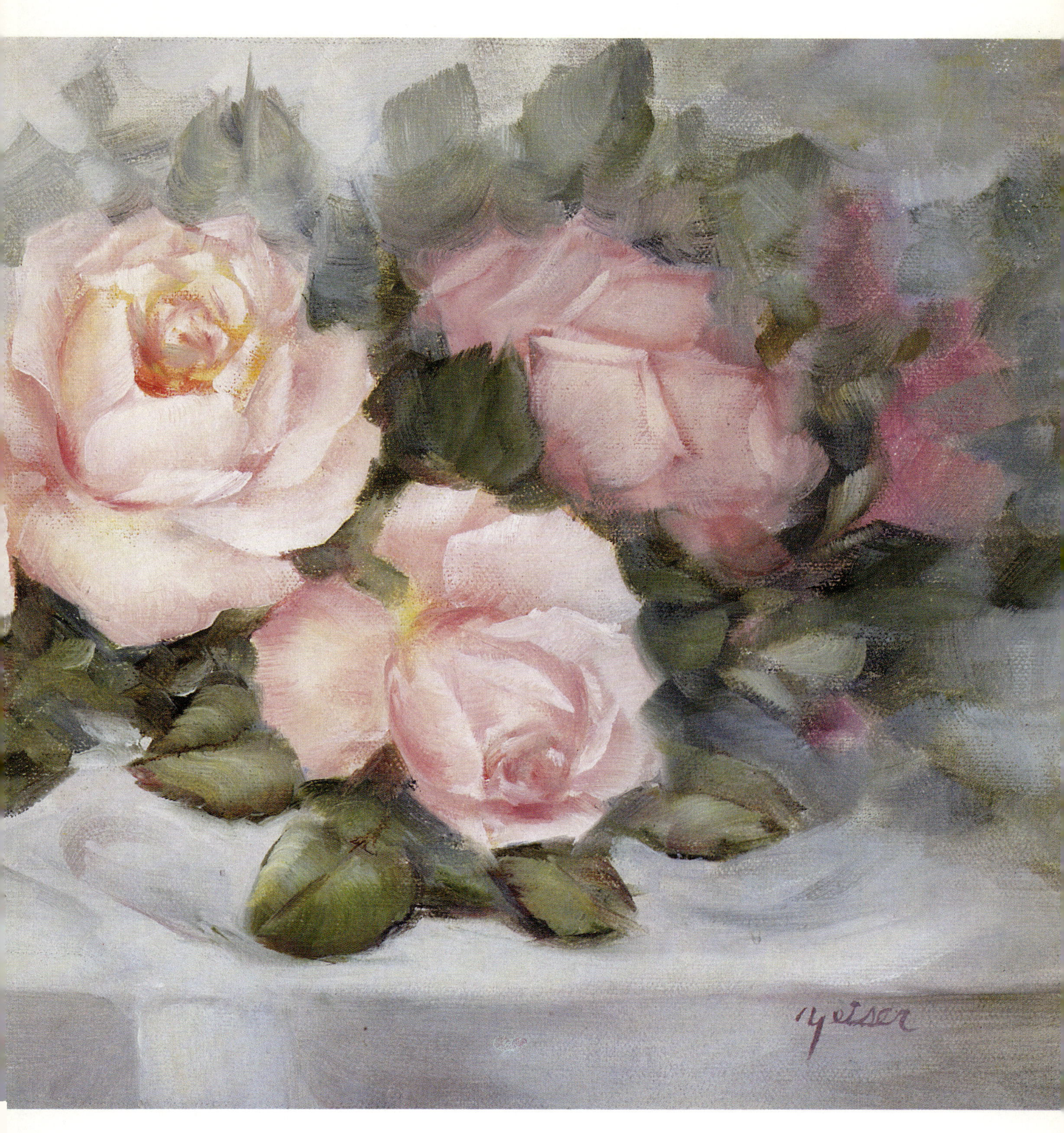

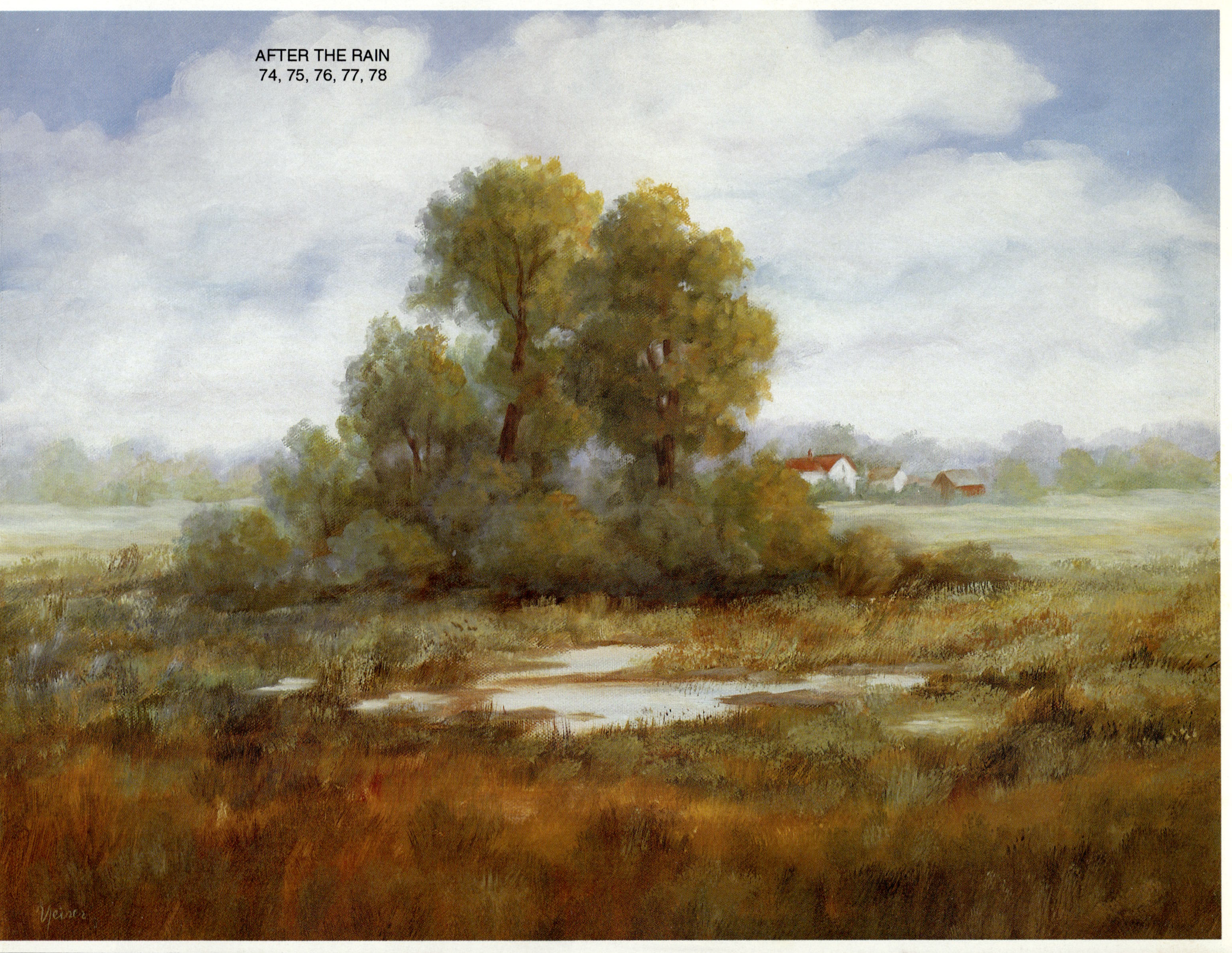
AFTER THE RAIN
74, 75, 76, 77, 78